9-1-2016

Dick + Nic,

I hope you'll enjoy
my Chapter 11 here and
give me names of all
you friends to whom
I can find a copy
of this book

Best,

Wells

MASTERS of SUCCESS

Published by CelebrityPress®, Orlando, FL.

CelebrityPress® is a registered trademark.

Printed in the United States of America.

ISBN: 978-0-9975366-1-4
LCCN: 2016940159

This publication is designed to provide accurate and authoritative information with regard to the subject matter covered. It is sold with the understanding that the publisher is not engaged in rendering legal, accounting, or other professional advice. If legal advice or other expert assistance is required, the services of a competent professional should be sought. The opinions expressed by the authors in this book are not endorsed by CelebrityPress® and are the sole responsibility of the author rendering the opinion.

Most CelebrityPress® titles are available at special quantity discounts for bulk purchases for sales promotions, premiums, fundraising, and educational use. Special versions or book excerpts can also be created to fit specific needs.

For more information, please write:
CelebrityPress®
520 N. Orlando Ave, #2
Winter Park, FL 32789
or call 1.877.261.4930

Visit us online at: www.CelebrityPressPublishing.com

MASTERS *of* SUCCESS

CelebrityPress®
Winter Park, Florida

CONTENTS

CHAPTER 1

MASTERING THE SKILLS OF PUBLIC SPEAKING

BY BRIAN TRACY

Whenever someone asks me how he can become a successful public speaker, I paraphrase to him the words of Elbert Hubbard, who said, "The only way to learn to speak is to speak and speak, and speak and speak, and speak and speak and speak."

But while it's true that the only way to become good at anything is by repetition, over and over until it becomes second nature, there are many things that you can do immediately to be more effective speaking in front of audiences of any size.

The dean of American public speakers, Dr. Kenneth McFarland, wrote a book titled, *Eloquence in Public Speaking.* In this book, a classic in the speaking industry, he did not talk about methodology or technique at all. His central message, which strongly influenced me when I began speaking publicly, was that the key to eloquence is the emotional component that the speaker brings to the subject.

To put it another way, the starting point to becoming excellent as a speaker is to really care about your subject.

I watched Wally "Famous Amos" give a talk to 1000 professional speakers in Anaheim a few years ago. He had started with little money and built up an extraordinarily successful chocolate-chip cookie business. Famous Amos Cookie stores sprung up all over the country, making him both wealthy and famous.

He then began to devote much of his time and money to helping people who are less fortunate, especially those who cannot read. His goal for this speech was to attract support for his charitable work.

He was clearly not a professional speaker and everyone was curious to see how he would make his presentation. But even without training or experience, his talk was absolutely excellent, and the reason was because he spoke from his heart. He spoke with a deep concern and compassion about the needs of people who couldn't read. He wanted to get across to the audience how important it was for everyone to be concerned about this problem, not only for the individuals involved but also for the future of America as a competitive nation.

Although his structure and his style may not have been as polished as that of someone who had spoken professionally for many years, he was eloquent because he really cared about his subject, and everyone listening could sense that emotion. He got a standing ovation that went on and on.

He demonstrated that the starting point of good public speaking is to pick a subject that is really important to you. You always begin by thinking about the experiences and ideas that have had an extraordinary impact on you, the information that you would like to share with others because you intensely feel that they could benefit from your knowledge just as you have benefited.

Let us say, for example, that you feel that people could be far more successful in life if they learned how to be more understanding of others. You have found, in your own life, that the more you worked at understanding how others were feeling, and where they were coming from, the more effective you became in interacting and communicating with them. Because of the impact that this knowledge had on your life, you feel that others could benefit from learning and practicing what you have learned and practiced.

With this, you have a springboard off of which you can leap into your first public talk.

The second part of public speaking is preparation. Preparation is more important than any other factor in speaking except caring about your subject.

Ernest Hemingway once said that to write well, you must know ten words about the subject for every word that you write. Otherwise, he said, the reader will know that this is not true writing. The reader would feel that this writing is shallow and insincere.

According to the experts in public speaking, to speak persuasively, the standard is much higher. You must know 50 or 100 words for every word you speak. Otherwise, your audience will have the sense that you don't really know what you are talking about.

THE IMPORTANCE OF PREPARATION

It's not unusual for a person to spend many hours, days and even weeks preparing for an important talk. I was once invited to give a 20-minute presentation to an elite group of top executives and politicians in a private meeting in Silicon Valley. Because of the potential importance of this talk, I did 16 hours of review and preparation. I read the minutes and reports from the previous meetings, and memorized the biographies of each key person. I planned my opening words carefully, and memorized them.

The executives did not know that the chairman, my client, was bringing in an outside speaker. When I was introduced to the group, I saw immediately that several of the attendees were not happy that I was there. Nonetheless, I smiled, scanned the group, and began.

As I spoke, I moved around, made eye contact, and quoted from things the various people had said in previous meetings. At the end of 20 minutes, I closed my talk by asking them to allow me to facilitate the rest of the meeting. The entire group agreed unanimously. It was a complete success. In thinking back, I was deeply happy that I had spent so much time in preparation. It was a turning point in my speaking career.

A MASTERFUL PRESENTATION

My good friend, Nido Qubein, now President of High Point University, once gave a one-hour talk to several hundred members of the National

Speakers Association in Atlanta, Georgia on the future of the speaking industry in the 21st century. The talk was scheduled for one hour. He concluded it in 59 minutes and 55 seconds.

Nido gave the talk without notes. He built the talk around ten key ideas and insights. He then developed each of the ten parts of the talk in a logical way, holding the complete attention of the audience. Each of the ten sections contrasted a pair of principles that involved marketing or sales or promotion. Each of those parts was thoughtful and detailed, and each idea was both insightful and thought provoking.

As he spoke, he walked back and forth across the platform. He gave specific examples and anecdotes to illustrate each point that he was making. He impressed me, and the entire audience, with the depth of his knowledge and with the thoroughness of his preparation.

He gave the talk as though he had given it 100 times before. He was extremely relaxed, genial and friendly throughout. He smiled and used body language skillfully to convey key points, and to illustrate and emphasize his key points. It was a beautiful example of professional speaking.

Later, in talking with Nido, I learned that, even though the talk was meant to be given only once, he had spent more than 100 hours of preparation, over a period of two to three months, getting the talk to the point where it was "just right."

FALLING ON YOUR FACE

A good friend of mine, a professional trainer, told me a story recently about a speaking experience he had had recently. He had been speaking on his subject for several years. He had become so confident that he had gone in front of an important business audience with almost no preparation for a half-day presentation. He felt that his knowledge of the subject would enable him to pull off the talk without anyone's realizing that he had not done the in-depth preparation that is necessary for that kind of a presentation. He did not fully understand the special situation, business and problems of this group.

To make it short, he told me the presentation was a disaster. Within a few minutes, he knew that he wasn't fully prepared. In a few more minutes, the audience knew that he wasn't fully prepared. They were both insulted and unresponsive. By the end of the first hour, the session had evolved into a series of critical questions from audience members, followed by challenges, disagreements and arguments that took up the rest of the morning. It was a terrible experience for him, and it was caused solely because he had neglected to prepare.

The next time my friend got a chance to make a presentation in front of a business audience, he spent every spare moment the week before fastidiously preparing and organizing. This time, he was ready. The presentation went off without a hitch. He received rave reviews and commentaries from the audience. Afterward, he told me that failing to prepare for the previous talk was one of the most valuable lessons he had ever learned. He would never again make the mistake of thinking that he could get by simply with knowledge of the subject.

PREPARATION IS THE MARK OF THE PROFESSIONAL

To prepare for a talk, the first thing you do is to write out an objective statement of what you wish to accomplish as a result of your presentation. Whether you are giving a 10-minute presentation or a six-hour presentation, the statement of your objective is the same. It is the answer to the question: "Who is my audience, and what effect do I want my talk to have upon them?"

Ralph Waldo Emerson wrote, "The aim of all public speaking is to move the listeners to take action of some kind, action that they would not have taken in the absence of the talk."

You need to ask, "What action do I want this audience to take as a result of the things I say to them?" Write out this statement of your objective clearly. Then write down everything that you think you could possibly say, one point after the other, to this audience to cause them to take this action. Remember, the reason for public speaking is not simply to teach or to share information. It's to move people's minds and hearts in such a way that they do something differently, that they change their behavior in some way.

DO YOUR HOMEWORK

Once you have an outline of what you want to accomplish and some of the things that you can say to accomplish it, begin to do your research. Gather information. Ask the meeting organizer. Go onto Google. If you don't feel that you have enough information, begin to read and to ask questions.

Another friend of mine, a top professional speaker, was asked to give a talk on something about which he felt very strongly, the importance of strategic thinking, but on which he had not done very much reading. He was amazed to find that it took him two solid weeks of reading and taking notes to gather enough information to give a one-hour talk on strategic thinking.

When you begin to speak professionally, you'll be amazed at how much work you will have to do, even on a subject with which you're relatively familiar, before you're in a position to speak fluently on the issue. Remember, you need to know 100 words for every word that you say. You need to have read at least 100 words for every word that goes into the talk that you give to an audience. If you've not done this quantity of research, both you and the audience will know very quickly.

WRITE IT OUT

If you're giving a short talk, the best strategy I have found is to write it out, word for word. Then read through it and edit it. Revise it wherever necessary. Add to it, and subtract unnecessary data. Work on it until it is polished, and then read through it several times so that you have such a good sense of the material that you can go through the entire talk prior to falling asleep or while you are driving your car.

Not long ago, I was invited to give a 22-minute keynote talk to an audience of more than 5,000 professionals. The organizers asked me for a written script of the talk, which they would carefully review and critique before giving me the go-ahead to put it into its final form for presentation to their audience.

Although I knew the subject intimately, it took me many hours to write and rewrite the script for the talk. I then gave the talk to a special audience of reviewers from this organization. They gave me about 20 ideas on how to expand or improve the talk in some way. I then rewrote the talk again and submitted it to them for their approval. Only then did I get the go-ahead to give the talk to the 5,000-person audience four months later.

OVER PREPARATION IS THE KEY

Once the talk had been finalized, I then reviewed it and rehearsed it more than 50 times. I need to memorize it so completely that I could give it from my heart rather than simply read the words from the teleprompter that they insisted I use to assure that there was no deviation from the approved texts.

The net result of all this preparation was that the talk brought a standing ovation from 5,000 people. Later, the organizers told me that it had been one of the very best talks ever presented to this group in 37 years of conventions that this organization had been holding.

It was no miracle. Every single additional effort at preparation eventually paid off. Preparation will account for fully 90 percent of your success in public speaking. You may not have the platform skills of a great orator, but you can be an extremely effective speaker if you do your homework and prepare thoroughly.

PRACTICE MAKES PERFECT

The first two parts of successful public speaking are caring and preparing. The third part is practicing. You need to practice your talk over and over, in front of friends and relatives and associates, and even in front of a mirror.

If you have an audio recorder or, even better, a video camera, record yourself giving the talk from beginning to end. Then listen to it or watch it, and make notes on how you could make it better. If you are videotaping your talk, look right into the camera and use the same facial expressions and body gestures that you would use if you were speaking to someone personally. When you critique yourself, be hard on yourself. Remember, the more honest and objective you can be about how you come across to others, the more effective you will be when you stand up to speak.

Practice makes perfect, and repeated practice makes it even better.

FROM THE MOUTHS OF CHILDREN

Let me tell you a story concerning my daughter Christina, who was 10 years old at the time. Christina was attending a private school near our home. The school wanted to add on a new building but was rebuffed by a neighborhood group that had gotten together to appear at a city-council meeting to loudly disagree with the expansion of the school. The members of the council had no choice but to suspend the application, neither approving nor disapproving it.

The founders of the school asked me if I would help them to prepare a presentation to the city council, to help them to make a second attempt to get the building permit. I told them that I would work with them but that the entire presentation would have to be very carefully prepared and organized in advance. Previously, they had just walked into the city-council chambers unprepared to face an entrenched opposition, and they had been defeated hands down.

While we were reviewing our strategy for the presentation, Christina spoke up and said that she wanted to get up and ask the city-council members to approve the permit. She actually wanted to speak at a public hearing. I told her that she could but she would have to write out her talk, word for word, and memorize it if she wanted to get a chance to speak.

TAKE IT SERIOUSLY

Before the week was out, she had sat down with her baby-sitter and my wife and written out a five-minute presentation. She then read and reviewed it, over and over, and prior to the city-council meeting, she was able to stand in front of the family and deliver her speech word for word without notes.

On the evening of the city-council meeting, various adults gave parts of the planned presentation and were quite effective. But perhaps the turning point in the entire process was when little Christina stood up on a chair behind the speaker's lectern and gave her talk, ending with the words, "Please pass this application and save our school!"

The reaction from people in the crowed city council chamber was incredible. Even though many residents of the surrounding neighborhood had gotten up to speak against the application, the city council voted to approve it. More than 130 adults, including representatives of two local newspapers, were in the audience. The following day, on the front pages of both local newspapers, Christina Tracy was written up—and quoted — as the 10-year-old girl who had swayed the city council into approving the application.

ADVANCE YOUR CAREER

Your ability to speak effectively in front of a public or private audience can do more to advance your career and increase your income than perhaps any other skill you can develop.

That being said, it is normal and natural for you to be nervous about public speaking. Fifty-four percent of American adults rank public speaking ahead of fear of death among life's major fears. Most people become nervous and uneasy at the very thought of standing up to speak in front of an audience.

Almost all people who can today speak fluently and fearlessly were at one time terrible public speakers. But they faced their fears and did it anyway, over and over, until the fear went away, which it always does.

However, you can overcome this fear, just as you can learn to type or ride a bicycle. You can take a course from the Dale Carnegie organization, or you can join your local chapter of Toastmasters International. These organizations help you with a process of what psychologists call "systematic desensitization." At every meeting, you get a chance to stand up and speak to a small group of other people who also want to learn to speak. Eventually, your fears go away and are replaced with confidence. Within six months, you'll be quite accomplished at selecting a subject, organizing your material and presenting the subject effectively within a specific time period.

JUST DO IT!

Speaking professionally is not really a skill that you can decide to develop or not. You don't really have a choice. If you want to realize your full potential in the world of business, you must learn how to communicate more effectively with groups of people. I have seen executives make extraordinary career leaps, saving themselves as much as five to ten years of time working up the executive ladder, simply by speaking extremely effectively in front of their peers at a corporate meeting. I've observed men and women who've put their careers onto the fast track by overcoming their fears and learning how to speak effectively before others.

Pay any price, spend any amount of time, overcome any obstacle, but make a decision, right now, that you are going to learn to speak well before groups. It could be one of the most important decisions you ever make in assuring long-term success in your career.

About Brian

Brian Tracy is Chairman and CEO of Brian Tracy International, a company specializing in the training and development of individuals and organizations. Brian's goal is to help people achieve their personal and business goals faster and easier than they ever imagined.

Brian Tracy has consulted for more than 1,000 companies and addressed more than 5,000,000 people in 5,000 talks and seminars throughout the US, Canada and 69 other countries worldwide. As a Keynote speaker and seminar leader, he addresses more than 250,000 people each year.

For more information on Brian Tracy programs, go to:
- www.briantracy.com

CHAPTER 2

WELCOME TO THE PLAYGROUND OF THE FEARLESS
– HOW TO BUILD A BILLION-DOLLAR BUSINESS

BY DAVE CARVAJAL

On track to become a big investment banker in the early '90s, Dave Carvajal spent two years at Prudential dealing with interest rate swaps, derivatives and risk management strategies. Ultimately realizing that he wanted to be in front of people and not spreadsheets, he decided to rethink his career path and leave investment banking behind.

Carvajal was drawn to an ad in the paper that read, "Life is tremendous! Come be a Superstar!" He thought it was hokey, took the bait and began working for one of New York City's top executive search firms. At 24, Carvajal wasn't even aware that the headhunting industry existed. He soon found he was the perfect fit. He learned everything he could about the business from 40 of the best and brightest headhunters. Working six days a week and making hundreds of Sunday calls 24 hours ahead of his colleagues, he became the company's top producer within eighteen months.

This set the foundation for a powerful career trajectory in the executive search industry. Carvajal hand-built HotJobs and TheLadders before becoming a hands-on builder of billion dollar businesses as the CEO of Dave Partners, a leading boutique executive search firm in New York's Internet, eCommerce and digital media industry. The firm has helped fill C-level leadership positions and assemble teams for major startups everywhere from New York City to San Francisco, Seattle and Austin. The firm's clients include Yahoo, Tumblr, Salesforce Buddy Media, Shutterstock and many others.

In the midst of the credit crisis of 2009, the entire headhunting industry was collapsing to a fraction of its size. Many top headhunters bolted for large corporate HR departments. During the chaos, Carvajal sensed an opportunity. He believed technology had the power to create the prosperity and abundance necessary to pull the U.S. and global economies out of the gutter. He also predicted that New York City would become a thriving metropolis for Internet and tech-enabled startups.

Fueled by these insights, he launched Dave Partners as both a capstone venture and a labor of love. His vision was to secure the highest caliber leadership teams for the companies that are building a better future for us all. As a result, Dave Partners has served as a key architect of the burgeoning New York technology ecosystem.

Over the years, Carvajal – now considered the top tech startup recruiter in New York City – has emerged as a world-renowned thought leader in the business of executive search. He is an expert on board formation and the building of world-class executive teams exclusively comprised of top 1% A+ executive leadership primed to conquer entire industries and markets. Dave Carvajal's firm has a dynamic cross-section of clients, from huge companies that rely on Dave Partners to build executive teams to smaller stage companies that Carvajal has helped develop and thrive.

"I know what it's like to grow companies that have had their eye on being the biggest in their industries," Dave Carvajal says. "With Dave Partners, that's not the focus. We don't need to be the biggest. We only want to be the best at what we do: the highest caliber executive search. We are often called the Goldman Sachs of executive recruiting—a boutique, white-glove services firm for the burgeoning Internet, eCommerce, and digital media space."

Carvajal's expertise has led him to create the framework that addresses the challenge inherent in recruiting the right A+ players as startups continue to grow and multiply. He believes the problem is two-fold:

1) To pry A+ players out of their current positions, you need a pitch that resonates with who they are and what they want to be – not just a pitch that is focused on money, perks, prestige, position and power; and

2) To find the right A+ player, you need to make a values match between the company and the individual, rather than a match only between the role specifications and an individual's skills.

Carvajal believes that by using a two-by-two matrix that consists of "You (the candidate) See/You Don't" on one axis, and "I (the employer) See/I Don't" on the other, recruiters can identify accurate and false perceptions and thereby make the right selection and avoid the wrong one. After contrasting perceptions, startups can winnow the list of candidates to a manageable number.

The two-by-two matrix will identify who has the technical chops essential for the job, but this is only 20 percent of what makes candidates successful in startups. 60 percent of success is figuring out if an alignment exists between a candidate's personal mission and values and those of the organization. He calls this set of conceptual models – Core Fit Process™.

Another core concept Carvajal distinguishes is the three levels of recruiting:

- Level 1 is Internet recruiting – posting a job online, receiving 5,000 applicants and figuring that one of them is bound to be perfect. This is a terribly ineffective way to find a leader.
- Level 2 is 'Referrals and Networking' – this often leads to mediocre candidates that are available and convenient, often left over from other search efforts rather than the highest caliber candidates. This may work for the big executive search firms but is less effective for high-growth startups.
- Level 3 is taking an elite, Special Forces approach to recruiting. Each search for a leadership position must be conducted with a fierce drive to find the ideal candidate.

"Level 3 recruitment means working harder than in the typical search," Carvajal says. "It means caring deeply about not only finding the right person, but communicating and listening to that person. It means presenting a powerful, irresistible argument to convince that candidate to leave his or her great job."

Carvajal calls this 'Extract and Secure.' "These guys are not between jobs, waiting for the phone to ring. They're already engaged in something they find interesting," says Carvajal. "It's about extracting them out of their existing state of even mild happiness just so we can put them through a filtering process and then secure the right executive for our clients."

"This is the highest and only level of recruitment worth talking about. It's about startups identifying the best 40 to 60 executives on the planet to come and be a chief executive *for us*," adds Carvajal. "Those two little words, for us, are critical because then it's about defining whether a candidate's personal DNA matches the cultural DNA of the company and its executive leaders. We start a process of defining and creating clarity around their own core values and competencies and figuring out who best suits the role."

Some of the most transformative, disruptive companies in the world have sought out Carvajal and his decades of experience at the forefront of organizational strategy, execution and executive leadership. In addition to his team's dedication and comprehensive, analytical approach to executive recruitment, another key advantage startups have found in working with Dave Partners is the firm's speed and efficiency.

The process of identifying, extracting and securing the top one percent of A+ talent can easily take the big firms 6 to 9 months because they are often encumbered with too many conflicts. Dave Partners can go through that process and achieve results in 2 to 3 months. "The big search firms are content with taking their time and moving slowly," says Carvajal. "But a few months of delay can be life or death for a high-growth company. Our ability to be agile and nimble and move at a rigorous pace is an important distinction. We pride ourselves on the white-glove service we provide in helping CEOs and entrepreneurs build companies the right way."

Dave Partners is often asked to go beyond the search partner relationship and advise its clients' board of directors as trusted counselors, as well as provide executive coaching and even strategic planning for executives. These extras ensure the wellbeing of the company.

Dave Carvajal paved the way for Dave Partners with his success leading two top Internet-based recruitment companies, HotJobs and TheLadders. With HotJobs, he had the opportunity to build a company that capitalized on the Internet's growing impact on the business world – a phenomenon he likens to the way TV profoundly disrupted radio's dominance decades earlier. In a nutshell, the company took the help wanted ads in newspapers and put them online. He ran the company's sales and launched a training program that needed only two and a half months to turn recent college grads into confident sales professionals. He hired their first 500 people and opened eight offices around the country.

As co-founder, he built HotJobs to 650 employees, $125 million in revenues, and $1.2 billion market capitalization after its IPO. The company startled the advertising world in 1999 when it bought a $1.6 million commercial during Super Bowl XXXIII. Yahoo ultimately bought HotJobs in 2002 for close to $500 million.

Explaining HotJobs' success, Carvajal says, "The five of us principals were strongly entrepreneurial problem solvers doing what had never been done before: inventing, creating, thinking and exercising sound business judgment and solving those issues faster, better and smarter every day. We fundamentally changed human behavior when it came to looking for jobs and made the task of HR professionals across the country that much easier."

Carvajal, whose humble beginnings include growing up in a tough neighborhood in Brooklyn, didn't know what to do after earning this windfall. He got married, started a family and spent a few years involved in real estate flipping properties – but being away from the day-to-day business world took a toll on his health. The doctor wanted to put him on cholesterol and blood pressure medications and told him to get in shape. He got healthy fast and discovered a passion for Ironman triathlons.

He then decided to team up with some of the guys he hired at HotJobs to build another company called TheLadders. In his five years there, he grew the company to 400 employees and $82 million in revenues. Just as with HotJobs, it became, as Carvajal says, "the hottest game in town" by 2008. TheLadders turned the HotJobs model on its head.

Whereas HotJobs was paid for by the companies looking for talent, TheLadders did the opposite with a consumer-driven subscription model. It took the search out of job search and served up to people a short list of high quality jobs relevant to their criteria for a monthly subscription fee.

"Although HotJobs, TheLadders and Dave Partners were and are very different companies serving unique needs, I can say that they have all taught me the value of finding just the right person to fill a position. I know from experience the skull-crushing pain, suffering and brain damage that comes from making a bad hire, and the complicated process involved in cleaning up that mess," says Carvajal. "I believe that there is an A+ player for every role in every company and every CEO should know this. All it takes is the right thinking and a little bit of hard work."

"From being on two Super Bowl championship teams and now thriving in this more targeted space with Dave Partners, I gained experience from making many judgment calls on a person's character. People trust me because I understand the root causes that make a company successful," Carvajal says.

Combined with his deep understanding of what drives high professional performance at many different kinds of companies, the foundation of Dave's success is also grounded in his love for people and his genuine interest in the daily work, motivation and high performance of the top executives who are solving humanity's greatest challenges.

About Dave

David F. Carvajal is an intrepid builder of billion-dollar businesses, a world-renowned thought leader in executive recruitment, and a man described as an "indefatigable force of nature." As CEO of Dave Partners, a bespoke recruitment firm serving the high-tech sector, Dave leads an elite, special forces recruitment team that extracts and places executive leaders that drive high-growth, venture capital and private equity-backed companies to unleash their full potential.

After a start in corporate finance in the early '90s, Dave quickly understood that securing and managing human talent was the key to value creation in a knowledge-based economy. In 1997 he co-founded HotJobs.com—and, in just under five years he power-built the fledgling startup to 650 employees, $125M in revenues, and a $1.2B market cap after its IPO. Yahoo bought HotJobs for close to $500 million in 2002. Dave then continued his success at TheLadders.com, swiftly building it to 400 employees and $82M in revenues.

Dave now consults with public BOD's, CEOs and startup entrepreneurs throughout the high-tech sector, advising them on executive recruitment and selection, organizational strategy, corporate values and leadership.

He founded Dave Partners as both a capstone venture and labor of love to help strengthen the workplaces that build a better future for us all. Dave Carvajal lives in New Jersey with his amazing wife, their twin sons and Clover the Wonder Dog.

- NYC's top tech/startup executive recruiter Dave Carvajal is a hands-on builder of billion dollar businesses.

- Following his success with high-growth enterprises HotJobs and TheLadders, Carvajal's Dave Partners works exclusively with the top 1% of A+ executive leadership.

31

CHAPTER 3

WHO SAYS YOU CANNOT HAVE IT ALL?
– USING SYSTEMS AND PROCESSES FOR PERSONAL AND PROFESSIONAL FULFILLMENT

BY CHRISTINA NGUYEN, HOMESMART PLATINUM LIVING

We can do more than we ever thought possible in life once we embrace who we are and identify our strengths.

"Christina, how do you do it?" This is a familiar question to me. To others, my life seems like it must be impossible to manage. **I have three young children, I am growing a Real Estate office of 50+ agents, sell about \$30M in real estate each year, and I still have time to enjoy my life outside of work.** Yes, I'm serious! I get to experience the joy of making memories with family and friends, never miss my kids important events, and unlike many people in the Real Estate industry—I rarely work on a weekend or over 8 hours in a single day.

When I first began a career in Real Estate, my life was like that of many agents that you've heard about. I had peaks and valleys, I worked weekends and made myself available to any lead whenever they needed me—regardless of what else I might sacrifice. This wasn't so bad back then because I was single and had no children. I could, quite literally, live for work. And it suited me well, because I embraced one of the biggest hindrances a person can have. I was a control freak. Today, I'm a recovering control freak, because *I've discovered the formula for finding the balance in life* that offers me professional success, but not at the expense of my personal fulfillment.

Letting go of my overbearing, control-everything style of self-perfection was so liberating, and it all began with this bit of advice that a systems and processes coach shared with me: *put the right people in place to do the things that are not rainmaking activities. This will free up your time to do what you are good at—and what you enjoy.* I took this to heart, as it was great wisdom. However, it was not necessarily easy to implement. It requires a change of psyche, which is something that most of us often resist at first, because it's habits and old ways that we must release. But I fought through it and it worked. If anyone were to ask me if it was worth it, it would take me only a fraction of a second to say, "Yes!" It was what spurred on the next question: **What is the highest and best use of my time?** It is from these ten simple words that my life has been formed.

BUILDING PROCESSES AND SYSTEMS THAT CULTIVATE SUCCESS

Building a successful business is not just about finding people to work for the business. You also need to create a business culture that works for your people.

Many of us have no problems putting in the time to achieve results in our chosen careers. This was certainly true for me when I committed to Real Estate over accepting admission into Dental School. I dove in and I worked really hard. It resulted in commissions, which kept me hungry for more. *The problem was that while I was riding on peaks, I was riding high, but then I'd hit the valley—that dip where the market is slow for whatever reason (economic factors or time of year).* And in those valleys, along with thousands of other real estate agents, self-doubt and shadows that make it hard to see the light, existed.

Striving for consistent business and the endurance to last for the long haul, I began to think about everything that I had learned through coaches, mentors, and self-education. *How could I take this valuable information and actually apply it to create processes and systems that would work for my needs, therefore my clients and agents needs, too?* To start the process, I evaluated two things, each one pivotal for defining how I'd achieve success and show others, through my actions, that you "can have it all."

1. **I learned how to hire the right type of people for the right job descriptions.**
   Our personalities dictate the fulfillment factor we will get from the jobs we choose to take. Finding the right job is important! Through learning how to evaluate people's passions and interests, I am able to put people into roles within my Real Estate company that fit their personalities. For example: someone who really loves to dive into all the paperwork that is a part of the industry, but doesn't enjoy the face-to-face interactions, can have a role working with the files for the clients we bring into the business. Together, we all work as a team and the results are phenomenal. Clients are being better served and taken care of, and the team understands their specific role and contribution in our success as a whole.

2. **I pinpointed the best systems and processes that would help with the goal.**
   There was a time in my life when I thought that in order to be respected and thought of as the best that I had to be the smartest one in the room. I'd learn and study and latch onto my desire to control a situation with all the strength I had. If an "i" needed to be dotted—I did it. If a "t" needed to be crossed—I was your person. Frankly, it was exhausting. Those small details were not my strength and they were wasting so much time that I wasn't devoting my time to what I did best—being the rainmaker for my business. By finding the right people to fill the roles that were extremely time consuming for me because they weren't in my wheelhouse, it opened up a tremendous amount of time for me to go out and generate the relationships I loved to create, and get new clients that I enjoyed connecting with, to do business with my team.

After I learned to rely on others for their strengths and began utilizing mine more, things got better quickly and it was noticeable. **Stress went down. Productivity went up. My time freed up.** Today, it's exciting to know that what I've tapped into is no longer just speculation and an educated guess—it's a proven method of systems and processes. I have not had to work weekends since 2008. That's nearly a decade of evidence that you don't have to do business like every other Realtor out there in order to experience success. And why would you want to?

TECHNOLOGY HAS CHANGED THE WAY WE DO REAL ESTATE

The value that Realtors bring to clients is different than what it used to be. It has changed the entire approach to building relationships and generating sales.

The benefits of the processes and systems that I have put into place have shown themselves in many ways over the years. The one that was interesting to experience was how beneficial it was for helping established Realtors maintain their value to consumers in a world where technology has given people access to more information on properties than they ever had before.

Once upon a time, a consumer would go out and look around at houses and see one for sale that appealed to them. They wanted to know more and they would reach out to an agent to find out the details of the property, including price, taxes, square footage, etc. Then they'd decide to look at that property or start working with an agent to find a property that would better suit their needs. This is a rare exception now. **Today, consumers have access to so much information about a property that they really have no urgent need to call a Realtor.** They know the property's history, its specific details, and lots of other information. *For many agents who'd built successful businesses, they froze at the changes that technology created in the way they do business.* It was overwhelming and left them with a few choices. Would they:

- Embrace technology
- Keep doing things "their way," even if it meant spending more time to earn less business
- Just leave the business, as it was no longer "what it once was"

If you don't embrace technology, it's safe to say that you've entered into a serious problem with your Real Estate career. It is a problem that I've effectively taken into account with the systems and processes that I've created. Agents who are great at selling but don't get the technology or have a team are taking note of HomeSmart Platinum Living, because we have a team that is excellent in this area—and it's a team that is willing to help others in this technology-driven world.

Agents who love the business but are lost as to how to change their current processes and systems—if they have any at all—are taking note of the way systems and processes lead to better business. In fact, when I decided on the HomeSmart franchise for my brokerage, I'd already taken into account how this business would support agents and appeal to them because of what they offered. This, in turn, helps to strengthen my ability to assist agents in cultivating their own success, plus helping clients achieve their objectives—whether it is to buy or sell a home, or both.

Objective #1: Teaching agents the value of systems and processes

A sustainable career in Real Estate today entails embracing: lead generations, winning presentations, and technology. Helping people step out of their comfort zone can be an exhilarating task, but when you know that you're on the right team that has the right systems and processes—and you have support—it becomes empowering and leads to results.

Objective #2: Create a Unique Selling Proposition

To best demonstrate what a Unique Selling Proposition is, I often refer to a Mercedes commercial that was highly effective. They showed this beautiful, luxury vehicle, and of course it was appealing. Then they tell you that you can get that for just $199.00* a month. Below, in small print are the details that are implied by that*. You don't have to know anything about Mercedes to understand that the price is a great deal for that car. People went to the dealerships in droves—to drive! The commercial got them to the dealership, which is its primary goal. Then, if the people loved the car they may go into negotiations on it. They'd mention the offer they saw on television and the sales associate would give them the details. If they didn't take that offer they maybe still took another one. Goal number two—a sale! This was Mercedes' Unique Selling Proposition. As a Realtor, what is yours?

I help Realtors determine what will make them different from all the competition that's vying for potential clients' business. It is not hard to get a Real Estate License, but it is hard to set yourself apart in a sea of thousands of competitors. We dive into these facets to create the Unique Selling Proposition:

- **How will you be a stand-out, as compared to a commodity?** Consumers have the information on the property now and repeating what they know will not set you apart. Thinking about what differentiates you from other Realtors and exposing those differences will set you apart.
- **Create headlines and put them in the spotlight.** Throw out bold ideas that draw consumer interest. Maybe it's a "If I don't sell your home in 120 days, I will buy it." Then, after you give the exciting headline, you show the details to back it up and tell them how it works. This helps to bring everything full circle, showing the consumer that they are a part of a team that knows how to deliver results.

Through identifying strengths, you can find your ideal spot amongst a strong real estate team, which means that you can find a home that you never want to leave. Not all agents move from company to company as a better offer comes along. You can tell a company that's as vested in agents as it is sales, quickly. There's this energy in the air and I'm excited to feel it and hear the positive buzz every day when I walk into my office. It's just another affirmation that things are working for all of us, because all of us are effectively using the systems and processes that will help us succeed.

KEEP GROWING TO KEEP GOING

Never assume that you've reached the pinnacle of success and you'll remain on top of the summit forever.

When we have clarity of vision, we have power and this is a message that I teach all of my agents through my business philosophy and the goal of the team that I've assembled. *It's growing quickly (50+ agent growth in just over a year) and we're keeping up with the demands, due to the systems that we've put into place.* **We all keep growing.** This is an important element of our systems and processes. We embrace a Tony Robbins philosophy called "Proximity is Power." *Through surrounding ourselves with amazing people who have excellent questions, we are all always the student as well as the teacher.* Knowing that so many people—whether they've only closed five deals in the business or they are veterans of the industry—have so much to teach me is incredible.

That desire to be the smartest person in the room and the control

freak have long since left me, making life so much better! Now I even take what I've learned about my professional environment and have taken it to my personal one. At home, systems and processes that work for a family of five are in place, making us be a stronger family unit. I don't have to repeat myself constantly, I know the questions to ask to have better conversations with my children, and those occasional challenging moments that all couples have become productive encounters where solutions are found. *We learn. We love. We grow. We strengthen our bond.*

Let's see…less stress at home and work, systems and processes that reduce wasted time at home and at work, and greater happiness and fulfillment both at home and at work. *I have these things, which makes me a very fortunate person.* And it is the evidence that with the proper insight as to what's important—what to hold on to and what to let go— that we really can have it all.

Our riches become the rewards of those we cherish and the clients we serve!

About Christina

Christina Nguyen's love of real estate began when she was just a little girl. She says, "I still remember the REALTOR® standing at the door with the keys to our new house. I remember how excited I was, thinking 'Oh my gosh! This is our new house!' For Christina, that passion never really waned, even though she had initially planned to become a dentist.

"I have a degree in biology. I'm wired in problem solving, and used to being in the lab. I planned to take that out into the world," she says. Yet, she couldn't shake the feeling that real estate was a better fit for her skill set, so she made a decision to try something that would allow her to give others that same feeling of excitement over their new home that she experienced as a child.

"I took a year break, and decided to dabble in real estate. I promised my mom and dad that if I didn't succeed, I would go to dental school," she says. However, in short order it became clear that Christina's love for a challenge and solving a problem would be more than fulfilled with a career in real estate.

"I jumped in with both feet," she says. "In this business you can't have one foot in and one foot out. I gave it 100% of my focus." To that end, she sought out training from the best sales professional she could find. Fortunately, a close friend was in high level management in the automotive industry. "He worked with BMW, Honda, Mercedes, all of them. He was a great negotiator, and he mentored me. I learned his style, and benefitted from his expertise in negotiating skills," she says.

Christina's track record speaks for itself. She sold 130 homes in one year in her career. Her homes earn 3.05% more than the average sales price in the area, and her listings spend an average of 36 days on the market in contrast to the average of 96 days on the market. Not surprising, she was recently voted the #1 individual agent for the number of transactions in her region by *Wall Street Journal/America's Best Real Trends* in 2013.

Yet, Christina still focuses on the client's own happiness in buying a new home, as her primary objective. In fact, she is so determined to help others to experience that same excitement about their new home that she recalls having as a child, that she offers remarkable guarantees for buyers and sellers.

"If my clients aren't happy with their home, I will sell it for free, or buy it back from them," she says. For sellers, Christina promises to sell their home – Guaranteed! If not she will Buy It.

"If they are not happy, I'm not happy."

CHAPTER 4

THREE STEPS TO OVERCOMING ROADBLOCKS

BY DAVID AUER, ESQ.

People struggle from time to time, whether in business or their personal life. They may be facing a roadblock or their career is at a standstill and they just cannot move forward. My story is addressing the person who has faith or is a person of faith. You may be someone who feels that you have come to a low point in your life, or even with your faith. You are starting to wonder what your purpose is and what you are really meant to be here on earth for. If, however, you are someone who has been fortunate and blessed with everything going well in your life; if you are someone who has never struggled and had obstacles or failures, this story may not be as meaningful. I am addressing that someone who feels like they hit that wall, or have that ceiling of complexity and have experienced either accumulatively or all at once a failure in their life that now they are at a stopping point.

I want to provide my personal experience and key factors of the journey that I have been on and still experience. I am not a product of a single dynamic event that propelled me to where I am today. I have experienced a ricochet series of experiences in my life hitting roadblocks that could have stopped me in my tracks. Each time after a period of meditation or pause, I restarted, reinvented or reignited my life or my faith, and had enough courage to build that momentum towards what I felt I was being led to do at that point. I would frame the key factors of what I have learned from this experience, not in any particular priority order, but maybe in a sequential order based on what happened in my life.

As I reflect on my story, I see myself as a slow learner. It took me several times to learn these key factors, and how to apply them in my life.

As a youth, my father was in the oil and gas industry, and we moved around quite a bit. I attended five different schools. As a result of that, especially during my formative years, I did not have the normal social base I think someone who might have stayed in one place would have had. I did not really have a strong foundation because of that. I could make friends quickly, but I was a troublemaker. However, I was blessed to have my grandparents who instilled faith into my life. In junior high, I was introduced to a straighter path: Boy Scouts. Today it may seem like an old fashion notion, but it, in fact, helped me get on the right track. What I learned in Boy Scouts, and what I am still learning being involved in Boy Scouts, is that they fill a void in young people's lives to help those young men go from being teenagers to being adults. For me, being around kids from my age and being influenced by adults and adult leadership, helped me learn life skills and how to work and get along together in a way you typically do not see in other environments.

So the factors I got out of Boy Scouts are to honor, have integrity and to be trustworthy. Ultimately building on my faith that I had, I was given life skills which helped me learn to get along with others, cease to be a troublemaker and learn to work together to achieve goals. Boy Scouts was an opportunity to stop ricocheting off one wall onto another and really try to find my way. I was pledging on my honor to do the best in everything I did. That was basically out of the Scout motto, and to always be prepared for what life presented you. Boy Scouts became an anchor that has stayed firm and established in my life over the last 40 years. My son just recently received his Eagle Scout award from the same Boy Scout troop I attended and received my Eagle Scout award as a youth.

Building on those key factors of honor, integrity, and faith, I was ready for the next challenge in my life. My love for sports introduced me to athletics. It helped me grow in hard work; working as a team member toward a common goal. I found my love for sports and athletics, and working together as a group, also built some other factors in my life that set the stage for me, preparing me for the trials that I was going to face later in life.

My parents were very big on education. My mother was a teacher and my father an engineer. I concentrated on getting an education and have built my career as a CPA, Tax Accountant, and Tax Attorney. I spent many years acquiring the education I needed to be successful in my field. I was set and on the road to success.

ROADBLOCK

I experienced a significant business failure in my practice as a CPA and an Attorney. This occurred over several years and was incredibly devastating from an emotional standpoint; financially it was very destructive. It's hard to explain the embarrassment and what appears to be a failure in life in general. I was someone who had gone through that much education and operated in the financial world. I had a failed business. It was a major roadblock.

I spent six months to a year questioning everything. Looking back, it was difficult to wake up every day and talk to people. The last thing I was going to do, as a fairly proud person, was find someone to help me. I was going to fix it or I was going to deal with it myself. In hindsight that probably caused me to be in that valley for a longer period of time than I otherwise would have been.

What started getting me out of that situation was going back to some of the things I had learned earlier in my life.

FAITH AND INTEGRITY

First of all, if I didn't have faith that God could help me get out of that valley, I think I might still be there. I also found that depending on my attitude; how I approached failure significantly impacted how quickly I was going to get out. What I learned in a lot of this soul searching and bible reading was, I realized that if God was teaching me something during that time period, I needed to be patient to listen to what it was. I learned the attitude that I needed to have, which did not come naturally, was to be joyful. I was going through this trial; this tribulation; this difficult time because it was teaching me something. I think at the end of the day what it was teaching me was how to persevere. I wasn't going to live a life that was absent of these hurdles or these roadblocks. I was going to need to learn how to persevere, and most importantly, trust and lean on God to help me get through.

As I circle back around, those factors of faith and integrity, to continue to be willing to work hard and persevere, those factors seemed to have served as stepping stones for me to not only get through the various hard times of my life, but also has created an expectation that if I consider it all joy every time something like that happens to me again, and if I look at it as a learning experience, my failures are only going to fundamentally strengthen me going forward in the future.

HONESTY AND INTEGRITY

In the journey I feel like I am on right now, as a CPA and a Tax Attorney, I come across a large number of people, especially business owners, who are at that point of hitting that wall. I feel like I am better equipped to help them as a friend, than by offering them my professional services. Encouraging them to be able to have the right perspective and to be able to continue to persevere through whatever they are struggling with.

THE THREE STEPS TO OVERCOMING ROADBLOCKS

1. Restart

I make relatively very quick decisions once I have information to go on. If I hit a major roadblock, I may tend to sit back and reevaluate and look at and question, "What is my overall goal? What do I really want to achieve?" I lived my life by trial and error and learned by moving forward rather than sitting still. I still tend to make quick decisions and continue to try to find ways to overcome whatever roadblock I am in the middle of hitting.

My mentoring style has become more as a colleague than as a boss. I tend to ignore the fact that I have more experience or knowledge or have ownership in the business. I look at whomever I am working with as someone I am working alongside and we are trying to achieve the same goal.

2. Re-Invent

Education: I had always put a lot of focus on education and becoming really good at what I did. I learned after that major failure, I needed to go back and reevaluate everything I had learned. What was it that I really did well that I needed to focus all of my energy on. Because if it is what I did really well, then I could immediately create the most value in the business. I think the other parallel for that was somewhere along in my past I had assumed that for me to get from where I was to where I wanted to go, I needed to have a partner. But I realized after that recent failure, having partners just complicated it and slowed me down rather than allowed me more freedom to get where I needed to go. So from an educational standpoint, realizing that I didn't need a partner was a major learning experience for me.

Faith: It goes back to my faith in what the bible has said and there are two verses that I go back to. James 1:2-4 "Consider it pure joy, my brothers, whenever you face trials of many kinds, because you know that the testing of your faith develops perseverance. Let perseverance finish its work so that you may be mature and complete, not lacking anything." That's one verse that has really spoken to me when I've struggled and I've hit a roadblock and need to restart.

In Romans 5: 3-5 it says, "... sufferings produces perseverance; perseverance, character; and character, hope." So both of these verses have taught me that going through a difficult time leads to perseverance, and perseverance either more character or maturity, and that leads to hope and basically maturity. So I reached out to these verses and these have served as an anchor through difficult times.

Honor and Integrity: If you are not honest with yourself and you look first inside yourself; rather than complain and place blame on other people, other things and other circumstances; if you are honest with yourself and you accept responsibility for where you are and what has happened to you. It allows you to have a different perspective and a stronger focus in first trying to improve yourself, rather than attempt to change the circumstances or change other people.

Hard Work and Teamwork: Just as the two verses speak of perseverance...to me, perseverance is a synonym for hard work. It is continuing to push through in whatever those struggles are, and looking around to the people who love you and support you as being on that team of helping you be someone who perseveres. I don't think I would have been able to go through that battle by myself. I have a strong marriage and great relationships with my siblings, whom I drew much closer to during that time as well as a couple of close friends. I would not have been able to have done it without that teamwork. That teamwork was not with partners or business people, it was with family.

3. Re-Ignite

I am motivated and charged by quotes I generally read from the Bible, but this is one, which Benjamin Franklin said, "Things which hurt, instruct." I think that kind of encapsulates the concept of education and perseverance.

Yes, there will be a time when you go through painful times, but if your perspective is: "you are going to learn from it," then you are going to end up being better off for it as well.

About David

David Auer is the founder of **Auer Tax Group**, a national tax planning law firm; **Blue Ocean Strategies**, a business strategic planning group; and **The Advanced Planning Group**, a collaboration of multi-disciplinary advisors focused on tax, estate, asset protection, and business succession planning strategies for successful business owners, professionals, and high networth investors all over the world. His email address is david.auer@auertaxgroup.com.

David has over 30 years of experience as a CPA attorney, earned his BSBA and MS in Accounting from Oklahoma State University, his JD with honors from the University of Oklahoma College of Law, and his LLM in Taxation from New York University School of Law. He has the Personal Financial Specialist (PFS) and Chartered Global Management Accountant (CGMA) designations with the American Institute of CPAs. David is a Fellow with the Esperti Peterson Institute and a member of the Order of the Coif, Wealth Counsel, and The American Association of Attorney-CPAs.

David lives in Tulsa, Oklahoma with his wife, Julie, and their three children, Ellen, John and Emily.

CHAPTER 5

RESTORING AMERICA ONE FAMILY AT A TIME

BY GARY SIPOS, MBA, AIF®

Financial security is more about Financial Processes than Financial Products.

Most financial advisors focus on Financial Products—choosing the best stocks or mutual fund that they can find. I have found that Financial Processes have a bigger impact on growing and sustaining your wealth than chasing after returns.

Many Americans have found themselves where their finances have been anything but stable or reliable for nearly the past two decades. The market has shown its volatility, which in turn, has spotlighted many people's vulnerability to its twists and turns. It's frustrating and maddening to everyone because it portrays a false reality; a perception that financial health comes solely from how you choose to invest, rather than engaging in Financial Processes that reduce or eliminate unknown and unnecessary losses. This is where I come in and help by using Financial Process Optimization to get the full, detailed picture for my clients.

If you don't lose money by paying taxes you think you must pay but legally can avoid paying by using a better financial process, or by maximizing the economic efficiency of your existing assets, one can substantially increase their wealth over their lifetime.

These Financial Processes cultivate relationships with people, while

49

working to help them avoid the uncertainties that come from simply relying on market performance alone. Yes, market performance plays a role and is important for growth; however, preserving what you gain is equally important. One might even say that it's critical. Realize that people lose money—their life's work—**unknowingly and unnecessarily**, by not knowing that Financial Processes exist, and thus not engaging in and optimizing them.

HOW THE PROCESS BEGAN

Working hard to earn money, just to lose it due to the market, will never feel or be "acceptable."

I am a second generation American who has seen a great deal in my life. I had grandparents who came from Hungary, each pursuing different paths to live out their hopes of achieving the American dream. They all landed at Ellis Island with nothing, and my mother's father became a millionaire by his early 30's, and my grandpa on my father's side was a simple, hardworking man who worked in the Pennsylvania coal mines. I believe that I've developed a few of their best qualities.

Growing up, I admit that I was forced to wonder why life was as hard on my parents as it was on occasion. My mother suffered from mental illness which didn't surface until after she was married, and my father was a good, kind man who worked hard, but wasn't able to help me with my math after fifth grade. Life was tough, and I had a temporary home in a car a time or two, but we never gave up.

My perceived hardships were motivation for growth and ensuring that I created something better for myself and the life I wanted to live. These situations helped me commit to the hard work and dedication it took to help ensure that my adult life wouldn't be as tough for me as my parent's lives were for them.

For starters, I had a strong focus on education. I was determined to make the most out of what was available to me—even if it appeared as a far reach. I worked hard, first attending Brophy College Prep, where I worked as a janitor to pay for my education. This helped me get into Loyola Marymount, where I continued working and benefiting from scholarships and a night job so I could earn my degree in Electrical Engineering with a minor in Computer Science.

After graduation, I was recruited by the CIA, but passed on that, thinking that I could accomplish more in life if I wasn't worried about being shot. It was exciting to see behind the CIA's black flag, but that choice, while honorable, just wasn't for me.

I ended up at Hewlett Packard. While working for HP, I enrolled in Stanford's graduate school of Electrical Engineering and it was there, out of all places, that I began to learn about the importance of Financial Processes and their substantial financial impact on your wealth.

Economics was my elective of choice and anytime I could take a class in it, I always did. Everything about it interested me and it led to one of the most memorable moments of my life, my "claim to fame," if you will. *My economics professor returned my paper and said he'd been up until the wee hours of the morning discussing my thesis with Milton Friedman.* Anyone who knows economics knows that is a name to be respected. I was so excited and I mentioned that I couldn't believe that Milton Friedman knew my name and that he'd read my paper. My professor instantly put me back into line by saying, "He does not know your name; he knows your paper." Nonetheless, that knowledge excited me and it was the kick-off to a serious interest in economic and financial processes, a fortuitous seed planted at Stanford.

After making "decent" money from my Silicon Valley start-up companies it was time to invest those funds. I thought I knew a lot, because I read financial magazines and followed Wall Street. What I realized was that my financial advisors "suitabilitied" the heck out of me. They sold me products that were in their best interests, not mine. They were just glorified stock pickers and did nothing about my Financial Processes to help grow my wealth. **A few struggles later, I realized that if it happened to me—a guy who knew a lot—it also happened to many Americans.** I wanted to change that and I ended up transferring over to a career that would highlight and educate people on the importance of **Financial Process** *over* **Financial Products.**

WHAT SETS SIPOS FINANCIAL APART

We educate our clients on the endless non-intuitive financial processes—each one designed to preserve first, and then grow their assets that they've worked so hard to achieve.

If you consider your financial life in pie graph terms, it looks something like this:

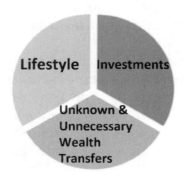

Most advisors focus only on the investment section. This puts much stress on growing your circle of wealth by focusing on only one section. *Where most people are unknowing, and financial advisors are unwilling to go is the third section of that pie chart*—**Unknown & Unnecessary Wealth Transfers (UUWT)**. This is where we start first. It's similar to a leaky bucket. Wall Street says pour more water in to fill the bucket. We say, plug the holes first, then even if your contributions are just a trickle, sooner or later your bucket will be full.

You cannot grow your entire circle of wealth if you only focus on one section.

There are endless financial processes including: your retirement funding process; your retirement withdrawal order; your capital purchase process; and your mortgage payment process. Know it isn't the mortgage you choose, but your paying process that counts. If you're retired, do you know why you chose your funds withdrawal order the way you do? Without knowing "why" you cannot learn "how" you can do these things more smartly. **This is all common sense stuff, but it's not taught nor implemented enough elsewhere.**

THE PROCESS OF CREATING YOUR TAX-FREE RETIREMENT

Most people fund their retirement with IRAs, 401(k)s, Deferred Compensation Plans, etc. But who really controls those retirement monies? The U.S. Government controls it because they can raise taxes. The more money you have in your retirement plans the more you risk when its withdrawn. Uncle Sam can raise tax rates whenever and as high as he wants.

Convert your IRA into a Roth IRA, tax-free, then you keep control of your money and not worry what congress does with tax rates.

You create your tax-free retirement by rolling your IRA into a Roth which causes a tax due, but then you establish a charitable trust that creates a tax-credit which offsets the IRA to Roth rollover tax. **Now your retirement money grows tax-free and is withdrawn tax-free.** In retirement, you live off your Roth and trust assets and when you pass away the remaining amount in your trust will go to charity, so replace your children's inheritance gifted away with a Wealth Replacement Trust. **This financial process typically adds millions of dollars to your estate over your lifetime using your same monthly cash flow. This does not affect your current lifestyle, just plugs a tax hole in your financial bucket to increase your lifetime wealth significantly.**

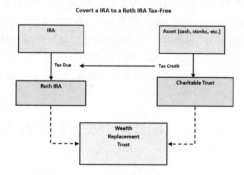

Covert a IRA to a Roth IRA Tax-Free

THE PROCESS OF ASSET PROTECTION

Protecting your assets is imperative to your financial well-being.

Most people are familiar with Living Trusts and they may even have them in place. That's great, but one thing that most people don't realize about them is that a Living Trust **will not protect your assets from predators and creditors.** Imagine this scenario...

> Mary's husband passes away and left her two million in life insurance. What her husband didn't plan for was that drunk driver who rear-ended her, sending her spinning into an innocent family. That family sues and gets twenty million. The catch: the jury says 90% of it is the drunk drivers fault. 10% is Mary's fault. Suddenly she owes two million dollars simply because she was in the wrong place at the wrong time. In an instant, her two million "nest egg" is gone.

What could Mary have done to avoid this? She had a Living Trust and it still happened. *What she really needed was something that is not used nearly enough: An Asset Protection Trust.* This would have protected what she owned, not just saved on avoiding Probate costs. If Mary and her husband would have had someone vested in Financial Processes, they would have received the protection they thought they had.

Always remember that asset protection will vary depending on the state you live in. Don't just assume you're covered. Know you're covered!

Another important function of asset protection lies in clients understanding the distinct difference between an umbrella policy for liability protection and choosing the smarter, more assured route of an Asset Protection Trust. Umbrella policies tend to put a bigger target on your back, because attorneys are very good at seeking out people with money. When's the last time you ever heard of someone with nothing getting sued?

THE PROCESS OF RETIREMENT DISTRIBUTION

Some of the solutions to smarter retirement withdrawals are easier than we may think.

All financial solutions do not lie in exchanging out investments, or replacing one for another. Imagine this scenario...

> Daniel is a widower and all his kids are grown. He has five accounts, each with different tax treatments and return rates. There's the

usual: an IRA, a ROTH, a Money Market Account, Savings, Bonds, and some dividends from investments. He is curious to know how long his money will last him, exactly. When he asks about it, he receives bad news—well, bad if he'd like to live past the age of 78, because that's when his money will run out with his current distribution method.

Daniel's situation is neither rare nor unique. *What he, along with others in the same situation, will never find out is that there is a way to make that exact same money, in those same accounts, last Daniel until he's well over 100 years of age* **with no additional risk**. This is how we discovered the good news—the better financial process:

By running an algorithm, we were able to determine that by withdrawing those funds in a different order Daniel would increase the years of his retirement income. We didn't change investments to do this, the Rate of Return (ROR), tax treatments, etc. **All we did was adjust the withdrawal order to recognize a very significant impact.** Daniel was unknowingly and unnecessarily transferring wealth out of his pocket simply because he was withdrawing his retirement funds in the wrong order.

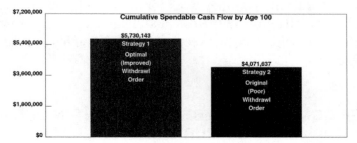

THE PROCESS OF BETTER HELPING OTHERS
Offering help and a financial legacy to heirs is an important motivator for many people.

One of the greatest things that parents and grandparents like to offer is the gift of paying for education. Imagine this scenario…

You find out that you're about to become a grandma for the first time, and your daughter is having twins! You've always wanted to pay for your grandchildren's college so you set up accounts so you can do that. A popular account for this type of grandparent gift is a 529 plan. You're setting up two and each one is going to have $25,000 in it.

Now ask yourself: Do you know for certain that this is as beneficial to your grandchild's education as you believe it to be? **Secondary education is a slippery slope for many people.** The department of education code is as intensive and hard to understand as the tax code. Basically, it's over most peoples' heads, including those who created it—Congress! With the 529 plan, the $25,000 each grandchild receives is considered an outside scholarship, which means their college scholarships are significantly reduced. If Grandma would have set up the 529 accounts under the mother's name, its impact would have been highly reduced, or using a better process may have meant no impact at all. It all comes down to the process chosen. Choose wisely.

Another way to have a better process for secondary education lies within how parents structure their accounts when applying for college aid. For example: business owners can often *not include* many business assets in their net worth, making it easier to get financial assistance. The catch is that most parents do not realize this and most financial aid officers are not going to tell them — as they work for the school, not the parent. I've helped clients realize this in the past and it came from my commitment to processes and helping clients keep as much of their hard earned money as possible.

WE ARE COMMITTED TO BEING DILIGENT IN OUR GOALS TO OUR CLIENTS

Nobody should lose their assets unknowingly and unnecessarily.

Through a focused, dedicated commitment to **Save America One Family at a Time***, we have made a difference in people's lives, giving them the opportunity to live independently and not rely on the need for government subsidies.* This is motivating and exciting. It makes it easy to go to work every day, because our goal is clear and precise. *This mindset is the heart behind Sipos Financial and the success we've gained and continue to create.*

By knowing Financial Processes, and clients' root needs and situations thoroughly, we offer solutions that significantly impact our clients' lives. I'm a fortunate man, because I know that regardless of what the market is doing on any given day I don't have to worry about calls from scared clients. **I've got them covered, and that's an inspiring thought—one that I enjoy waking up to and going to sleep with every night.**

About Gary

Gary Sipos, MBA, AIF® helps you create a tax-free retirement using advanced financial processes. Most families unknowingly and unnecessarily transfer wealth out of their wallet. Our financial process approach substantially increases your wealth as opposed to simply chasing after stock returns.

There are hundreds of financial processes with one example being converting your IRA to a Roth IRA using advanced processes that make this a tax-free conversion. Another financial process example is a retiree withdrawing money from their accounts. Most retirees have a Roth, an IRA, bonds, a taxable account, etc., and those accounts all have different rates of return, risk levels, and tax treatments. Withdrawing money in the wrong sequence can cost you tens of thousands or millions of dollars over your lifetime. Our financial process shows you your optimal withdrawal strategy that maximizes your retirement estate value.

Other process includes the process of funding your retirement plans, paying your mortgage, or purchasing cars, etc. We are not referring to a better product (the mortgage, the stocks, etc.,) but are referring to better financial processes that have a significant impact on your overall wealth.

Gary started his career in Silicon Valley, starting at Hewlett-Packard and then founding multiple companies, some that became listed on the NASDAQ or were acquired by larger public companies.

While in college, Gary worked as an engineer designing the AH-64 Apache helicopter for the U.S. Army. After college Gary was recruited by the Central Intelligence Agency, but even though it is a noble path he decided to move to Silicon Valley where he said he was less likely to get shot.

Gary is the author of *College Cash Solutions*, and co-authored *Masters of Success* with Brian Tracy. Gary was a featured advisor in *Elite Advisor Magazine* and has been seen on NBC, ABC, CBS, and FOX.

Gary graduated from Loyola Marymount University with a B.S. in Electrical Engineering and a minor in Computer Science while playing in the scrum of the four-year undefeated Southern California divisional championship Loyola Rugby team. He earned an M.B.A. from St. Mary's College and was a Stanford University Masters candidate in Electrical Engineering before leaving early for his first start-up.

Gary holds a series 65 investment adviser representative certificate, has earned the

Accredited Investment Fiduciary® (or AIF®) professional designation awarded by the Center for Fiduciary Studies associated with the University of Pittsburg. Gary also earned his California Insurance License: # 0G63835.

Gary and his wife, Dr. Lisa Harpenau, live in San Francisco, CA., with their standard poodles, Arthur, Rey, and Henry. Gary lists Biblical research, chess, 1959 Corvette restoration, volunteering through the Kiwanis organization, and an inordinate amount of dog walking as a few of his favorite activities. Gary's self-confessed claims to fame are he once played two-on-two beach volleyball with Karch Kiraly, played the drums at The Fillmore, and once had his econ paper critiqued by Milton Friedman. All those events made his day!

You can connect with Gary at:
- Gary@SiposFinancial.com
- www.SiposFinancial.com

CHAPTER 6

MARKETING YOUR MISSION

BY JW DICKS, ESQ. & NICK NANTON, ESQ.

He thought it was absolutely the most disgusting thing he had ever seen in his life.

To most people, having a mammoth company like McDonald's invest heavily in your company would be a godsend. To Steve Ells, it was a necessary evil. Although he had built his fledgling "fast-casual" restaurant chain to a modicum of success – a total of 18 locations - he needed more capital to truly create a full-fledged nationwide franchise.

The problem was that he viewed the restaurant business through a completely different prism than the Golden Arches. They wanted him to put in drive-through windows and he refused. They wanted him to serve breakfast – again, he refused. He insisted on using high-quality ingredients and they upbraided him on costs, saying that, proportionally, he spent as much on food as a classy steakhouse. That made him laugh. All he sold were burritos.

Now, McDonald's was out to school him by sending him to their chicken farm in Arkansas, where they sourced much of their poultry – and he was appalled by what he saw.

The experience cemented his business mission in his mind. He returned and told his staff he wanted to change the way the world eats. He created a Mission Statement that centered on the words, "Food with Integrity," and worked to increase their use of naturally-raised meat, organic produce, and dairy without added hormones.

McDonald's thought he should at least use his efforts as a marketing wedge – the execs wanted him to put the word "fresh" in the name of his restaurants. His response? "That's a bunch of (expletive deleted). Why would we do that? It doesn't make any sense."

After a few years, McDonald's realized Chipotle was not a very good match with the huge multinational and divested itself of Chipotle's stock. That was fine with Ells – by that time, his chain was up to 500 restaurants and more and more investors were clamoring for stock. But he did need to market the business in a powerfully effective way in order to keep revenues rising. So, Ells hired an established ad agency to help them make a nationwide impact with their marketing. Unfortunately, he got the typical slick advertising advice, same as he got the typical fast food advice from Mickey D's. He quickly fired the agency.

Because Chipotle did food its own way, he thought the marketing should be just as unique – so he took the whole operation in-house and hired a Chief Marketing Officer to target the audience he thought was Chipotle's path to true success - millennials. Millennials believed in the kind of food sourcing principles that Ells did and would pay a little more to support those principles. But Ells had to get the Chipotle message out to them in a way that was trustworthy; millennials didn't fall for the usual traditional media marketing – they felt it was inauthentic. Ells' conundrum was that Chipotle needed some traditional media to reach the largest possible audience.

The answer came in the form that, ironically, was 100% millennial – YouTube.

Ells had commissioned an animated short to be created called "Back to the Start," which featured country music legend Willie Nelson singing Coldplay's song, "The Scientist," about going back to basics; the cute and appealing two-minute film focused on a farmer's journey from running a huge industrialized farming "factory," much like the McDonald's one that had offended Ells, to engaging with more sustainable and humane practices. It garnered a terrific reception online and was quickly and heavily shared through social media.

That was just fine with Ells, who felt "Back to the Start" perfectly captured the Chipotle ethos. He wanted as many people to see it as possible. To that end, he thought about running the entire two-minute short during the Super Bowl – but the price for that ad placement would have been higher than the company's entire media budget for the year. Finally, they decided to run it during the Grammy ceremony in 2012 – they figured the blockbuster music telecast of the year would deliver more of their target audience anyway.

The strategy was a success. Ells continued to produce similar shorts about responsible farming and food sourcing. They were able to actually lower their media budget over the next few years, because their targeted marketing was so effective.

The student truly outdid the teacher. While Chipotle experienced skyrocketing profits and success, expanding to over 1800 locations and topping $4 billion in sales in 2014, McDonalds' net income in 2014 fell by 14%.

Chipotle's success truly came from finding an authentic company mission and, just as importantly, marketing it effectively. In this chapter, adapted from our new book, Mission-Driven Business, we're going to break down how Chipotle created Mission-Driven marketing campaigns that had the maximum impact for the minimum cost – and how you can put the same processes to work for you with your business.

YOUR MISSION MARKETING TARGETS

With any kind of marketing, it's important to zero in on certain targets. With Mission-Driven marketing, it's essential. When you have those targets in your sights, your marketing will allow you to bond in an authentic and powerful way with those who share your mission – a bond that has a strength that goes way beyond any conventional marketing.

If you can hit all, or even most, of the following five targets, you'll quickly attain that kind of bond.

Target #1: Your Audience
How well do you know your audience? If the answer is, "Not very well," then it's time to dig in deep and get acquainted.

Hopefully you've taken our earlier advice and chosen a mission that will appeal to your most likely buyers. This is a crucial alignment that needs to be in place. As already discussed, Chipotle did, in fact, already have a desirable target demo in mind as it moved forward with its enormous expansion: Millennials. And they made a perfect choice in that regard.

Millennials (those roughly 19 to 36 years old) act differently than their predecessors, the Baby Boomers, and many brands, like McDonald's, have been slow to understand and take advantage of that difference. Chipotle wasn't. In fact, they knew they were in the exact right place at the exact right time to meet the Millennials' specific eating preferences.

Millennials wanted to turn away from the traditional fast food giants, because of the constant downgrading of food quality to keep profit margins high and prices low – but they still needed a high-value, low-cost place to eat, and Chipotle was there to fill the bill. But, as the chain expanded to mammoth heights, marketing was required to deliver the Chipotle message to potential customers in new locations. That marketing had to continue to appeal to millennials.

According to research, there are three main strategies that work best when it comes to the millennial mindset:[1]

1. Appeal to the values that drive them: Happiness, passion, diversity, sharing and discovery.
2. Understand their realistic lifestyles and experiences and find ways to enrich that realism.
3. Make sure they feel informed and involved, not just marketed to.

Chipotle absorbed these strategies and used them to fuel their Mission-Driven marketing, as you're about to see. Understanding their target audience was the critical first step to formulating an effective marketing plan – and it should be your first step as well.

Target #2: Your Message
Here's a well-worn, but very valid proverb: It's not *what* you say, but *how* you say it. That's never truer than when it comes to crafting your mission's marketing message. Once you've established what your target demographic is and researched its mindset, the next step is to move on to crafting a marketing message that lines up with your mission as well as

your demographic's tastes.

Here's how Chipotle did it. As noted, millennials scorn traditional marketing and would rather feel informed and involved. Chipotle was smart enough to acknowledge that fact and make their marketing much more about its mission than its actual food or restaurant experience. By using the "Food with Integrity" tagline, the marketing message immediately elevated the quality of its offerings in the public's eye and also cemented support for healthier farming practices. It also avoided making empty marketing promises that millennials would reject as a cliché. For example, imagine if Chipotle claimed they served "Tasty Food with Integrity" or "Delicious Food with Integrity," the kind of language most restaurants would insist on having in their advertising? It would have diluted the effect. By making the tagline a seemingly-simple declaration of fact, however, Chipotle showed its marketing integrity to millennials.

So - how can you sum up your organizational mission in just a few words? A few words that will have the proper impact with your audience? What kind of language will work best with your target group?

Target #3: Your Media
There's a reason you see all those bladder control commercials on TV newscasts – it's because those shows are the most effective way for those companies to reach older viewers, who make up the overwhelming majority of the audience for such channels as Fox News and CNN. They purposely picked media that would deliver them the biggest audience that would be receptive to their pitch.

Now that you have your target audience and messaging in place, it's time for you to do the same. The good news is, thanks to the Internet, there's never been so many different options for marketers to explore in the history of mankind. When you're choosing where to deliver your message, however, it can be just as important to *avoid* certain media as it is to choose the right ones.

Case in point, Chipotle's media strategy. From the get-go, Chipotle wanted to avoid the traditional fast food TV advertising that might cause the company to be lumped in the same category as other chains it was anxious to differentiate itself from. Instead, it embarked on a low-cost high-impact strategy using primarily alternate media to connect with its target audience.

Beginning with its "Back to the Start" short, the company continued to seek out nontraditional marketing media to post its mission-oriented content, using music videos featuring Karen O of the Yeah Yeah Yeahs and Willie Nelson, another animated short called *The Scarecrow* that linked up with a mobile video game, and a four-part original Internet series entitled, *Farmed and Dangerous* on Hulu.com, which was a satire of "Big Food" practices. All of these videos and products featured very little actual marketing of Chipotle beyond being branded with its name – yet all strongly supported and furthered its "Food with Integrity" mission.

Perhaps more importantly, all of these projects gained Chipotle a ton of free publicity and goodwill on a very small budget. As Marc Crumpacker, Chipotle's Chief Marketing Officer, puts it, "We're trying to appeal to an audience we call the 'conscientious eaters.' Those people are already pretty loyal, but we're trying to resonate with people who aren't thinking about that much. They don't have to choose Chipotle, ultimately. But we'd love for them to think about where their food comes from." [2]

So think about what sort of content will best deliver your Mission-Driven message – and which media will best deliver that content to your demographic.

Target #4: Your Authenticity

Many have found marketing can be a very slippery slope when it comes to promoting a mission. Any whiff of blatant self-interest will destroy a carefully-crafted marketing strategy within seconds on social media if you're not careful.

We'll turn to our old friend McDonald's again to demonstrate this hard fact of life. The burger giant attempted to solicit heartwarming tales from its customers in 2012 by creating the Twitter hashtag, #McDStories. What followed was a torrent of abusive tweets from, you guessed it, millennials who replied harshly with these kinds of comments:

Dude, I used to work at McDonald's. The #McDStories I could tell would raise your hair.

One time I walked into McDonald's and I could smell Type 2 diabetes floating in the air and I threw up. #McDStories

These #McDStories never get old, kinda like a box of McDonald's 10-piece Chicken McNuggets left in the sun for a week. [3]

We don't mean to pick on McDonald's, but it's clear their marketing perspective isn't as sharp as when it knew how to sell itself like no other brand did. The fact is, it's way too easy for a business to set itself up for ridicule with botched Mission-Driven marketing – the public is just waiting to pounce.

How do you avoid that? By running a business that supports your mission's principles – and by always being consistent and truthful when marketing that mission. To do otherwise, as you'll see in the next chapter, can fatally compromise your credibility and even your entire brand.

That's why you should always expect your Mission-Driven marketing to be challenged – and you should always be ready to take on that challenge.

Chipotle actually wasn't. When it produced its "Back to the Start" video, the company viewed it as a broad-based fable of sorts, not to be applied specifically to Chipotle itself. However, since it had the Chipotle name on it, viewers viewed it as Chipotle making promises about how it sourced its food. That led to a complaint to the Better Business Bureau, who asked Chipotle to prove they practiced the processes preached in their video – and luckily, Chipotle was able to pass that test and be given the BBB stamp of approval.

Know this: If you can't back up your Mission-Driven marketing with facts, if you're exaggerating or being disingenuous in any way, you will take a hit down the line. The power of being Mission-Driven derives from being truthful and genuine; once you violate those principles, you're in trouble. So it's best to be aware, even if you believe you're just passing on information, you're still creating expectations about your organization. Even the Red Cross takes a lot of heat for the way it spends revenues from donations.

As Chipotle CMO Crumpacker said of the BBB experience, "One of the things we learned is to be very truthful and accurate in the things we're doing...while we think we're telling a simple story, the people watching it are taking a lot away from it, and if you're not careful they may take something away that you weren't expecting. You don't want people turning against you." [4]

Target #5: Your Community

With Mission-Driven marketing, you don't want to just talk at people – you want to talk with them. That means seeking out and even creating opportunities to connect with the community that supports your mission.

Chipotle understood this principle, as did Ben & Jerry's before them, and focused on finding ways to interact and bond with their community in fun, relevant and educational ways that weren't preachy or tedious. Instead, the intent was to create an ongoing dialogue that's both socially aware and entertaining.

For example, over the past few years, the company has held a series of free "Cultivate Festival" outdoor events that draw tens of thousands of people. The festivals hook up attendees with local unique foods and beverages under the Chipotle umbrella. It has also launched a "Cultivating Thought" program by adding printed content to its bags and cups from such high-profile writers as Toni Morrison and Malcolm Gladwell, and even cutting-edge comics such as Sarah Silverman.

Now – think about your organization's mission. How can you best reach the people who will respond to it the most strongly? What other local (or national) organizations can you team up with who also support your mission? And what interactive events and in-store (or in-office) methods can you use to further connect with your base? Remember to always try to make your mission a two-sided conversation, instead of a lecture.

WILL YOU HIT THE BULL'S-EYE?

As we hope we've made clear in this chapter, when you're moving forward with your Mission-Driven marketing, you should have a clear idea of how to present your mission in a way that will make your potential customers respond in the strongest possible way.

That means you must clearly understand every angle of your campaign, including...

- **Who you're talking to**
  Once again, know your target audience thoroughly – their behaviors, their opinions and their attitudes towards marketing.

- **What you're talking about**
  You yourself have to understand your own mission thoroughly in order to carry it out effectively - both its advantages and its disadvantages.

- **What makes your mission unique**
  What is it about your mission that makes it different from other organizations' – and how can you best exploit that difference to make people stand up and take notice? How can you take advantage of that difference in your marketing?

- **Why your mission matters**
  You have to sell your mission to your audience – which means you have to understand what makes it important to them. Chipotle, for example, continually promotes the fact that their food-sourcing improves their menu items' quality and adds extra value to their meals (which makes the slightly-higher prices justifiable).

- **What makes your mission authentic**
  How is your mission reflected in how you do business? Is there any aspect of your business that undercuts that mission? If so, how do you account for that? This is an issue you MUST resolve before engaging in Mission-Driven marketing.

- **Why Mission-Driven marketing may not be enough**
  While Mission-Driven marketing certainly packs a punch, you may also need to do more traditional hard-sell tactics to support your organization. This is a fact of life even Chipotle has to face. Of Chipotle's non-traditional marketing strategy, restaurant marketing veteran Dan Dahlen says, "Chipotle will eventually get to that point, that to drive same-store sales they'll have to go to TV. As you get into the top spenders in the category, there's a correlation between share of voice and share of stomach."[5]

Even Chipotle's CMO realizes that day is coming – but the company is putting it off for as long as possible. "The alternative is to switch to the type of marketing that every other fast-food company uses - with these new menu items and big ad campaigns to promote them. Once you get on that model, I think it's very, very hard to get off. I want to try to do this as long as I can."[6]

And remember - once you commit to Mission-Driven Marketing, you have to stay committed or risk a significant backlash. By persuading consumers to believe in your mission – and your dedication to it, you're generating a great deal of good-faith loyalty. And the last thing you want to do is create a firestorm of outrage by breaking with that faith.

[1] Spenner, Patrick. "Inside the Millennial Mind: The Do's & Don'ts of Marketing to this Powerful Generation," Forbes Magazine, 4/16/2014

[2] Morrison, Maureen. "Chipotle Bucks Fast-Food Convention While It Still Can," Advertising Age, March 12, 2012

[3] Hill, Kashmir. "#McDStories: When A Hashtag Becomes a Bashtag," Forbes, 1/24/12

[4] Morrison, Maureen. "Chipotle Leaps Forward With 'Back to the Start'," Advertising Age, November 26, 2012

[5] Morrison, Maureen. "Chipotle Bucks Fast-Food Convention While It Still Can"

[6] Morrison

About JW

JW Dicks Esq., is a Wall Street Journal Best-Selling Author®, Emmy Award-Winning Producer, publisher, board member, and advisor to organizations such as the XPRIZE, The National Academy of Best-Selling Authors®, and The National Association of Experts, Writers and Speakers®.

JW is the CEO of DNAgency and is a strategic business development consultant to both domestic and international clients. He has been quoted on business and financial topics in national media such as the *USA Today, The Wall Street Journal, Newsweek, Forbes, CNBC.com,* and *Fortune Magazine Small Business.*

Considered a thought leader and curator of information, JW has more than forty-three published business and legal books to his credit and has co-authored with legends like Brian Tracy, Jack Canfield, Tom Hopkins, Dr. Nido Qubein, Dr. Ivan Misner, Dan Kennedy, and Mari Smith. He is the resident branding expert for Fast Company's Internationally-syndicated blog and is the editor and publisher of the *Celebrity Expert Insider,* a monthly newsletter sent to experts worldwide.

JW is called the "Expert to the Experts" and has appeared on business television shows airing on ABC, NBC, CBS, and FOX affiliates around the country. His co-produced television series, *Profiles of Success,* appears on the Bio Channel - along with other branded films he has produced. JW also co-produces and syndicates a line of franchised business television shows and received an Emmy Award as Executive Producer of the film, *Mi Casa Hogar.*

JW and his wife of forty-two years, Linda, have two daughters, three granddaughters, and two Yorkies. He is a sixth generation Floridian and splits his time between his home in Orlando and his beach house on Florida's west coast.

About Nick

An Emmy Award-Winning Director and Producer, Nick Nanton, Esq., is known as the Top Agent to Celebrity Experts around the world for his role in developing and marketing business and professional experts, through personal branding, media, marketing and PR. Nick is recognized as the nation's leading expert on personal branding as *Fast Company Magazine's* Expert Blogger on the subject and lectures regularly on the topic at major universities around the world. His book *Celebrity Branding You®*, while an easy and informative read, has also been used as a text book at the University level.

The CEO and Chief StoryTeller at The Dicks + Nanton Celebrity Branding Agency, an international agency with more than 1800 clients in 33 countries, Nick is an award-winning director, producer and songwriter who has worked on everything from large scale events to television shows with the likes of Steve Forbes, Brian Tracy, Jack Canfield *(The Secret, Creator of the Chicken Soup for the Soul Series)*, Michael E. Gerber, Tom Hopkins, Dan Kennedy and many more.

Nick is recognized as one of the top thought-leaders in the business world and has co-authored 30 best-selling books alongside Brian Tracy, Jack Canfield, Dan Kennedy, Dr. Ivan Misner (Founder of BNI), Jay Conrad Levinson (Author of the Guerilla Marketing Series), Super Agent Leigh Steinberg and many others, including the breakthrough hit *Celebrity Branding You!®*

Nick has led the marketing and PR campaigns that have driven more than 1000 authors to Best-Seller status. Nick has been seen in *USA Today, The Wall Street Journal, Newsweek, BusinessWeek, Inc. Magazine, The New York Times, Entrepreneur® Magazine, Forbes, FastCompany.com* and has appeared on ABC, NBC, CBS, and FOX television affiliates around the country, as well as on CNN, FOX News, CNBC, and MSNBC from coast to coast.

Nick is a member of the Florida Bar, holds a JD from the University of Florida Levin College Of Law, as well as a BSBA in Finance from the University of Florida's Warrington College of Business. Nick is a voting member of The National Academy of Recording Arts & Sciences (NARAS, Home to The GRAMMYs), a member of The National Academy of Television Arts & Sciences (Home to the Emmy Awards), co-founder of the National Academy of Best-Selling Authors, a 16-time Telly Award winner, and spends his spare time working with Young Life, Downtown Credo Orlando, Entrepreneurs International and rooting for the Florida Gators with his wife Kristina and their three children, Brock, Bowen and Addison.

Learn more at: www.NickNanton.com
and: www.CelebrityBrandingAgency.com

CHAPTER 7

THE ART OF WEALTH CREATION FROM RENTAL PROPERTY

BY KORIANNE MAR

Introduction:

Have you ever noticed that when you are doing something you enjoy time seems to fly by? Conversely, when you have a job that you don't like, the time drags and you spend all of your time staring at the clock waiting for the day to end. I didn't want to spend my entire life watching a clock and hating my work, so I decided to pursue a new career, something that I could truly enjoy.

I went into the rental business, and it has been my passion for more than 15 years now. Being happy at work is something that I am deeply grateful for.

I am so blessed and pleased to share the knowledge that I've gained with you, and I hope you employ my strategies to help you on your own path. It can help you to build your financial future, and many of you might find that it is a potential financial vehicle that you can use to build a business – so you can finally quit that day job that has you sitting and staring at the clock.

Before we get into the details of using rental properties to create your wealth, I want to let you know more about me and my journey that brought me to this point. It's a long story, but I believe it serves to illustrate problems and concerns that many of you are probably facing right now.

WHAT WAS I DOING BEFORE?

You might be wondering what type of job I had before I made the transition to rental properties. Well, I was working in the high tech industry for a few years before the last company I was working at shut down because they ran out of funding.

That is one of the dangers of working for someone else, especially in a field that has that sort of risk. You don't have control of what happens, and you might come into the office one day to find that the company you work for has been sold, or in my case, didn't have the funds to keep going.

It's scary.

When I was out of work, I decided that there was no way I was going back into the corporate world. It wasn't something I enjoyed, and there was no future there for me. Let's go a little further back in time, though, so you can get a better understanding of why I made the decisions that I did.

I thought back to the time when I worked for 3M. I had a little cubicle that I called "home" while I was at work. There were four co-workers who were seated in the same area, and they had an average of 20+ years of experience. In fact, one of them had been there for more than 30 years.

Even at that point, while at 3M, I would come home from work and think about what would happen to me if I were there for 30 years. Would I enjoy that type of life? My heart and my mind were both brutally honest with me and answered with a resounding "No!"

WHAT I DECIDED TO DO

I was very fortunate that I had a husband who was very supportive of my decision to make a career change. We didn't have any children then, so I was able to take the time to figure what my passion was going to be. After about three months of searching, I settled on finance. I knew that I would enjoy it since I liked working with numbers and I liked working with people.

At the time, I didn't know much about the field, so I decided to train. For three months, I trained extensively with an experienced mortgage broker who had been in the business for more than 30 years and who was getting ready to retire. He taught me the ins and outs of the business, and after training, I got my license and opened up a mortgage company.

I was very excited that my business took off after about eight months, and I was able to earn a six-figure income. That's not to say that it all came easy, though. It was a lot of hard work and long hours that I spend learning to run and build a new business. I didn't mind the hard work, though, because I was determined not to go back into the unpredictable corporate world.

THE FIRST RENTAL AND BEYOND

Due to the success of my business, my husband and I were able to increase our savings and even buy a new house. We made sure it was in the best school district we could afford, because we knew we wanted children down the road.

When we bought our new home, we didn't sell our old one. Instead, we became instant landlords by turning it into a rental. Even after all of the expenses were paid, we were able to see a positive cash flow of $500 a month. This was passive income, and I really liked the idea of that!

Next, I took a three-day real estate investment training course. This was in 2001, and I paid $7,900 for the course. I felt it was well worth it though since it would provide me with more knowledge and more skill to advance into the real estate business. I enjoyed the training enough that I decided to sign up for six months of private coaching.

While I was at the three-day seminar, though, I was lucky enough to meet a very knowledgeable builder. He was at the event with the goal of finding high net worth investors who would be interested in investing in his master senior community that would be going into Paradise Valley, Arizona.

At lunch, he presented his plan and said that he wanted to have $500,000 from each investor to join the senior community master plan. The plan involved building 100 homes, each of which would be in the $400k to $500k range.

I explained that we did not have $500K. I didn't have enough to invest in the project, but we did become good friends afterwards. He was the one to advise me to sell the rental property and to use the equity to buy five more properties that would be able to generate $1,700 a month rather than the $500 a month we were getting from the single rental that we had at the time.

I took his advice.

Let's look at the numbers so you can see how it all worked. They might seem a little confusing at first, but once you go through and read the rest of the chapter, everything will make more sense. For now, these can give you a good sense of how things can progress.

With the $230,000 in equity that we had, we were able to put 20% down on five new rental properties that we bought.

Purchase Price: $200,000
Down Payment: $40,000 (20%) + $6,000 (Closing cost)
Loan Amount: $160,000 @ 6% (30 year fixed-rate mortgage)

Rental Income: $2,000
Mortgage Payment at 6% = $959
Tax = $300
Insurance = $100
Vacation Rate (5%) = $100
Maintenance (5%) = $100
Property mgmt. fee = $100
Total expenses = ($959 + $300 + $100 + $100 + $100 + $100) = $ 1,659

Rental Income: $2,000
Total Expenses: $1,659
Monthly Cash Flow: $341/month
Equity Pay Down: $159/month
Cash on Cash Return: $341 × 12 months = $4,092/year

$4,092/$46,000 (down payment + closing cost) = 8.8%
This return does not count the equity payment of $159/month in the mortgage payment.
From one property we had produced $500/month.

Now with five properties, each of them produced: $ 341 × 5 (rentals) = $1,705/mo.

In 2001, from one rental sold we purchased five rentals.
In 2002, we purchased two more rentals from our savings.
In 2004, we refinanced our seven existing rentals and took money out (cash out refinance). Most of the properties were valued between $270K and $320K, and we bought them for between $200K to $220K.

We were able to do a cash-out refinance for $53K for each property.
$300K × 80% = $240K (new loan amount)
$60K less $7K Refinance Closing Cost = $53K cash back

$53K cash × 7 Properties = $371K

Our initial capital: $230K (2001) + $92K (2002) = $292K

Now we put $317,000 in our savings that we did not have to pay for capital gain tax. We again used this money to reinvest in other real estate rentals that produced monthly cash flow. In 2005 we bought ten more cash flow properties from a builder at 20% below market value.

I loved the mortgage business and helping my clients, but I had less interest because I worked average 12 hours/day and missed a lot of quality time with my first son. I decided the mortgage business was not the right business for having a family. So, my career focus shifted to the rental business in 2008. Since then, profits from the rental business has exceeded that of my mortgage business.

From 2008 to 2011 I bought over 40 projects from bank owned, foreclosures properties, wholesale investors and asset managers at deep discounts. I also fixed/flipped about a dozen projects, but found out the fixed/flipped strategy did not meet my financial objectives of return on investment for the amount of time and effort that I put in.

Throughout these past 15 years, I still love the buy and hold strategy because it meets my objective of producing *monthly cash flow* and it builds wealth for our retirement in the back end because the equity is paying down for the loan amount that we owe, and maybe gains some appreciation when the economy is in the expansion phase.

At the same time, I gain the most tax deduction benefits yearly. I now work 12-15 hours per week on the rental business managing the property managers and helping them to screen new tenants because of my strong underwriting background from the mortgage business. I know how to access risks based on the tenants' income, credit history, and monthly debt payment, etc.

On a side note, we lost 80% value of our stock/bond account when the stock market crashed in 2000. After having all our assets once in the stock/bond market, it becomes easy to see that owning rentals that create passive monthly cash flow is a much better choice for us, because we know the return on the investment is tremendously rewarding and predictable based on the economic data that we research in an area before investing. Rental properties are hard assets.

WHAT THIS INFORMATION CAN DO FOR YOU

This introduction is to serve as an inspiration and a reminder to you that you don't have to stick with your day job if you don't enjoy it, and it's one that isn't helping you to make any money. When you are able to generate your own wealth and create a steady flow of passive income, you are in charge of your life.

I am proof that it can be done.

My vision for this book is to help ordinary people like myself build wealth buying one rental at a time using a safe-buying strategy that I laid out in this book for you to follow from start to finish. I also want to save you a lot of money from paying for real estate seminars that offer outdated information, and most of the presenters are not active investors themselves.

I share with you all my wealth of knowledge that I have been using for the last 15 years so you can implement it and buy your first rental and figure out whether it is the right financial wealth creation for you and your family.

Some of you may even use it build it as a business while you still have a full time job, so you can be financially independent sooner than working on a corporate job. Think about it, you have to work five months just to pay for federal/state/social security taxes. You only bring home seven months of your yearly salary. How much do you have left after all your monthly expenses? Is your job providing enough savings for your retirement?

How much sooner can you retire if you just buy one rental a year? By year 10, you will own 10 rentals and each of them will produce $400/month. This will bring in $4,000/month cash flow.

Can you quit your job with that monthly income? If not, what can you do to save more so that you can have money for a down payment for a new rental purchase?

It is time for you to create financial independence for yourself so you can focus on doing things that you love and things that matter most. **The real estate rental business has created a balanced life for me and I know it can do for you as well.**

About Korianne

Korianne Mar is a proud mom, wife, entrepreneur, world traveler and philanthropist.

She was raised in Vietnam under a strict dad, who flew her out of Vietnam alone when she was in her late teens, seeking freedom and opportunity called the American Dream. She came to America and worked non-stop to improve all aspects of her life, because she has a strong desire to live a well-balanced successful life with joy. She always reminds herself that she is a life-long learner. She worked two jobs to put herself though college and finished with a double major and no student debts.

After graduating from college, she landed an IT job at 3M, but her job was not challenging enough, so she left to find another opportunity that would keep her challenged. She landed another job with a high tech startup, which offered her a 40% pay raise, but 10 months after joining the company, it closed its doors because they ran out of money. Instead of getting another job, she refused to get back into the corporate world; though her experience, she knew that she would not enjoy working in a corporate job for another 30 years of her life, and missing out on a lot of interesting life experiences, but the biggest thing was TIME to spend with her kids and family. She knew that working for someone else would not provide her the freedom of time and create financial independence that she desired.

Seeking out a new opportunity to become her own boss, she found a new opportunity in the finance sector, specializing in residential mortgages. She founded her own mortgage company after three months of extensive training with an experienced mortgage broker of 35 years. She closed over $150 million in residential mortgage loans. While running a successful mortgage company, she also started building a rental business for her family focusing on residential investments. She knows that one day if she and her husband are no longer able to work for any reason, there is a business that can support her family. By 2008, her real estate investments provided her financial independence, so she withdrew from the mortgage business.

Korianne started out buying just one rental property and then grew it into a rental portfolio of 45 projects at one time. During the last 15 years of her real estate career, she has bought/sold over 90 rental projects. She is now spending time managing rental projects in six different regions around the United States and is still actively selling/buying when an investment makes sense.

Korianne enjoys spending time with her family travelling around the world 3-4 times a year. She is an avid fitness fanatic, loves outdoor activities and is a consistent donor for humanity and homeless kids' projects.

Visit her website for information on *The Art of Wealth Creation from Rental Property* book and additional resources on living a fulfilled and balanced life. (http://www.korianne.com)

CHAPTER 8

THE ONE-TWO PUNCH TO FINANCIAL INDEPENDENCE

BY LEASHA WEST, MSFS, CHFC®, CASL®, NSSA®, CLTC, MDRT

As more people fight to become financially independent, I'm frequently asked how to generate extra income – oftentimes by those living on fixed incomes and by others wanting to replace their income from their current job, or to spend time on more desirable activities. Is this you? If so, read on, this can easily be accomplished by delivering a financial one-two punch. The first punch is creating multiple streams of passive income and the second punch is knocking out debt once and for all.

To master success, you must understand active vs. passive income in order to achieve financial independence and hedge against a crumbling economy. Let's start by defining financial independence: this is when your current lifestyle expenses can be met with your

INCOME	
Active	Passive
Man-at-work	Money-at-work
Income received that you have actively worked for.	Income received which you have not actively worked for.

investment income – that is the goal. So, what is passive income anyway? Passive income is any income you receive from any activity that you are not actively working at - a residual income that pays without you being directly involved. This differs from active income which is income that you have worked for. Your salary, commission, and bonus are all active income that you receive due to services or labor that you perform. Active income will stop if you are ever fired, laid off, ill, or unable to perform your job duties; whereas passive income keeps on flowing regardless of your circumstances. And with a commitment to creating your own economy and becoming financially solvent, rest assured the benefit is worth the effort of developing passive income.

NOTE: I only share suggestions that I do personally; I don't feel it's ethical to teach or recommend anything that I don't do myself. So let's dive in, here's my top five ways to gain financial independence and generate passive income:

1. Rental real estate

Any rental property that can be rented and yields a monthly cash flow is a fantastic source for passive income. Out of my top income-generating activities, this is the most expensive but produces the most advantages. In addition to the monthly passive income, the tax advantages of owning rental property are immeasurable not to mention the appreciation over time. Traditionally, you may be thinking of rental property only where people live; however, if rentals are not your thing and you dread the thought of midnight phone calls, overflowing toilets and tenant drama, you can always hire a property manager and there are many other unconventional rental property opportunities to consider. For example, I own a few small parking lots which are very easy – cars pay or get towed. Explore parking lots, storage facilities and other rental options which can be done with no money down. Lastly, don't discount businesses or commercial property; as this can be lucrative in accumulating rental properties and building your passive income.

2. Intellectual Property (IP)

Another great source of passive income is intellectual property. Intellectual property refers to mental creations that are associated with legally-recognized rights, such as material that can be copyrighted, trademarked, or patented. This includes articles, books, music, movies, artwork, photographs, comics, software, logos, and more. For example, writing a book is a passive income stream, once your book is completed and published, you can begin receiving proceeds from direct sales or royalties from the publisher. You can also earn income by selling the associated movie and merchandising rights. Now, unless you're J.K. Rowling or John Grisham, passive income from writing books is not going to sustain you. The idea is to keep writing multiple books so that the income adds up.

Additionally, IP can include licenses for your creations or licensing other people's stuff. In a broader sense, you can license your intellectual property to other entities, who can then exploit it to generate revenue, and depending on how the deal is structured; you can earn a cut of that revenue. This is what happens when you sign a publishing deal with a book publisher. They sell the book, and you receive royalties from book sales. Don't let the word *licensing* scare you, licensing simply means "giving permission." Normally when you license work you created, both parties will sign a contract spelling out the terms. The possibilities are limitless!

3. Internet businesses

The internet offers a huge platform to carry out your own business, be it large or small. With a little bit of dedication, you can setup your very own online business with minimal investment to grow your passive income. A few ideas for the vast Internet business opportunities include starting and monetizing a blog, becoming an affiliate marketer, creating and selling gigs, offering virtual assistant services, social media consulting for businesses or opening your own eBay store. There are innumerable Internet business opportunities. I personally have several e-commerce stores, a membership website and sell online products.

Everyday, someone buys something from me that is drop-shipped in a fulfillment house and I get paid. This is an easy, cost effective way to create another stream of passive income. Find something that is interesting to you and that ignites your passion. You can do the same thing too.

4. Joint Ventures (JV)

If you're not familiar with joint ventures, it's best described as two or more parties undertaking a commercial enterprise while remaining distinctively separate, not partnering or incorporating. Normally, JV's are not long-term, ongoing business relationships but a single business transaction or collaboration; however, every deal is different. This is where your network comes in as the person with the relationship wins.

Top 5 Passive Income Streams

* Rental property
* Intellectual Property
* Internet Business
* Joint Ventures
* Hard-Money Lending

For example, people bring me deals that I triangulate. I make introductions, coordinate the parties and put the deals together with somebody else's money and somebody else's work. I'm simply the gal standing in the middle that structured the deal. This is a beautiful way to make passive income. A good place to start is identifying complementary needs either in your business or in another business where a joint venture relationship can fill a weak spot.

Maybe an ideal joint venture partner might have products or services that would enable you to stimulate additional, incremental revenues from existing customers and provide an additional magnet for new customers. Could both parties benefit mutually from the exchange of some form of shared marketing or distribution arrangements? Start exploring joint ventures, pay attention to the opportunities around you and get good at negotiating.

5. Hard-Money Lending (HML) or Peer-to-Peer Lending (P2P)

Ah, the holy grail of passive income. Collecting interest on money that you lend out should be the ultimate goal. If you're not familiar with hard-money lending, it's a little more involved but yields much higher returns to you – commonly in the double-digits. HML is typically individuals or small groups that lend money based on the value of property and not the borrower's credit scores. The loans cost much more than the average mortgage and carry high origination fees. When you develop relationships with developers and house-flippers, getting into HML enables you to help them quickly purchase properties, make some quick fixes to raise the property value, then get a new loan (based on the property's new, improved value) to pay off the hard money lender – you! For the most part, HML is based on short term loans.

If HML seems too risky for you, another option to consider is Peer-to-Peer Lending (P2P). This practice has recently come about by lending money to individuals or businesses through online services that match lenders directly with borrowers. Since P2P companies operate entirely online, they have very low overhead and provide this service more cheaply than traditional financial institutions; however, the lending intermediaries collect a fee and you receive the monthly payment until the loan is repaid - wash, rinse, repeat.

Fighting for financial independence takes more than just the daily grind relying solely on one job. No matter how much money you make, mastering true success includes developing other sources of income. The ideas are endless, find what interests you and take action now!

DEBT ELIMINATION – IT'S ALL ABOUT THE MATH!

Once the passive income starts rolling, it's time to knock out your debt. As you know, finances are the foundation of every household; yet, there is very little education about how finances work. Most people are left to make their best guess and get trapped under a pile of debt. Without education, they will continue to make the same mistakes over and over.

Creating financial security isn't about the mistakes you've made in the past. It's about creating a solid plan for the future, and utilizing tools to help you achieve the level of prosperity you deserve; all without requiring any change to your current income or checking your credit.

Determining the fastest way to pay off your debts is simply math. Yes, the big secret is math. Paying off debt in a fraction of the time can easily be done by using a program that has captured the banks' most profitable strategies, combined it with cutting-edge technology, and delivered in a system that is turn-key for the masses.

How is that possible? By calculating the various potential paths, including computing all of the variables associated with each debt and time value of money, and then mathematically determining which debt to target, when, and with how much – it's all MATH! I'm talking about a program called the **Worth Account.**

The *Worth Account* computes all the math into one program using advanced banking strategies which identify the fastest, most effective financial blueprint for your given situation. Following the program will eliminate your debt, build up cash reserves in your bank account, create an emergency fund and increase equity quicker. And, it's done in an extremely user-friendly program which you can access 24 hours a day, 7 days a week. This is a game-changer for mastering success and winning the fight for financial independence.

I've been on this program since 2010 and absolutely LOVE IT!! I will have my 26-year mortgage paid off in only 9.1 years and am over halfway there – I'm saving over $327,000 in interest and almost 20 years of payments. I did this without refinancing, my monthly payments remain the same, and there was no change to my monthly budget! You have to see how this program may help you and your family knock out debt!

By using the *Worth Account* program, there is no need for debt counseling, debt settlement, debt consolidation or bankruptcy, the program will guide you like a GPS for your finances, mapping out the fastest way for you to reach your financial goals and putting you on the path to living a debt-free life. (See bio for details.)

LIFE AFTER DEBT

You must plan for life after debt and your newfound financial independence to keep your spending in check. So what exactly should you do when you've finished paying off your debt? Sounds like a terrible problem to have, right? Think again, because we know how easy it is for money to disappear if it doesn't have a purpose. And with debt out of the way, you're no longer emotionally paralyzed or worried about overextending your finances. It's important to mentally prepare for new financial opportunities after debt and how you will responsibly manage the surplus.

A couple of months before the final payment, take some time to plan a meaningful purpose for your money. Once it sinks in you've got extra cash that you don't owe to creditors anymore, there needs to be a plan in place. For some, a debt-free life is a chance to live larger; for others, it's an occasional splurge. What will life after debt mean for you?

Now that you're suited up to win the fight for financial independence, it's time to step into the ring and begin the starting round. Hit the debt hard by starting your Worth Account and your passive income streams will grow that much faster. Stay disciplined and focused, and delivering the final blow will be a rewarding victory.

About Leasha

Leasha West, known as America's Retirement Authority™, is a highly decorated Marine Corps veteran and respected community leader. With the explosive success of her firm, West Insurance & Financial Group, Inc., she is now recognized as one of the nation's leading experts in retirement planning and insurance.

As an award-winning and multiple best-selling author, Leasha was selected as one of America's PremierExperts® and is frequently quoted in *The Wall Street Journal, USA Today, New York Times,* and *Inc.* magazine, as well as featured in several publications and news outlets commenting on retirement issues. She has shared the stage at distinguished conferences across the country with legends of business, Hollywood, politics and sports, including Arnold Schwarzenegger, Sylvester Stallone, Al Pacino, Steve Wozniak, co-founder of Apple, Eric Trump, NFL Hall of Famer and 3-time Super Bowl Champion Michael Irvin, Fashion Mogul Donna Karan, Oprah's life partner Stedman Graham, supermodel-turned-supermogul Kathy Ireland, George Ross of the Donald Trump Organization and Celebrity Apprentice, NY Times #1 Best-Selling Author Dr. John Gray, the lingerie tycoon of Europe, Michelle Mone, Wayne Allyn Root and the World's #1 Wealth Coach, JT Foxx.

Leasha's combined knowledge and celebrity status has solidified her as a retirement planning guru as she is frequently called on by local and national media for her ability to communicate, teach and transfer her innovative and rarified financial skills.

Leasha serves on the Board of Directors for numerous non-profit and for-profit organizations. As a result of Leasha's outstanding volunteerism, she was awarded the President's Volunteer Service Award by President Barack Obama.

In addition to her community involvement, she is a multi-year member of the Million Dollar Round Table, was named to the Circle of Excellence by the Women in Insurance and Financial Services (WIFS), and was chosen as one of North America's Elite Women in Insurance by *Insurance Business America Magazine.*

Educationally, Leasha holds a Masters Degree in Financial Services (MSFS) and the prestigious designations of Chartered Financial Consultant® (ChFC®), Certified Long Term Care (CLTC), National Social Security Advisor® (NSSA®) and Chartered Advisor for Senior Living® (CASL®). She is the spokeswoman for The American College.

Leasha has intensity, contagious enthusiasm and amazing passion for helping baby boomers, seniors, and retirees preserve and protect their portfolios, maximize their Social Security income, make sense of Medicare, generate income through solid cash flow and use of growth to offset inflation.

Through Leasha's strategies and inspiration, retirees are likely to avoid probate court and protect their assets, investments and savings from losses due to volatile markets, needless taxation or an extended illness. She has personally helped thousands of clients retire in the comfort of their homes rather than being cared for in a nursing home.

To get started with your Worth Account, visit: www.worthaccount.com/west or call 888-532-7429.

If you are retired or retiring soon, and would like to learn more about securing your retirement in any economy, visit Leasha's websites:
- www.westfinancialgroup.com
- www.americasretirementauthority.com

You can connect with Leasha at:
- leasha@westfinancialgroup.com
- www.twitter.com/LeashaWest
- www.facebook.com/LeashaWest
- https://www.linkedin.com/in/leashawest
- https://plus.google.com/+LeashaWest

CHAPTER 9

MASTERING PASSION
– THE STARTING POINT OF ALL SUCCESS

BY MOUSTAFA HAMWI

One-way ticket out of Dubai!

Do you really know what makes you tick?

Without knowing the answer to this question you will feel like something is missing no matter how successful you are; which is how I felt many years ago while I was running multi-million dollar businesses in the entertainment, modeling and events industries in Dubai.

The more glamorous my life became the more empty I felt, and that made me realize that making an enormous amount of money while being unhappy is failure! Most of us while in pursuit of happiness lose sight of our ultimate destination and get stuck in the rat race for more money, and there is never enough money!

It became increasingly apparent that having clarity on one's passion and purpose affects more than just direction, it impacts the quality of life!

My journey to find meaning took me on a one-way ticket to India in 2012. In the Himalayas, **I met a Swami who had been meditating in caves for 13 years**. During one of our interactions he asked me, **"What are you really thirsty for? Only when you know what you are thirsty for can you quench your thirst!"** As I did not have an answer yet I decided to spend months with him in meditation, yoga and introspection; and during this long period three questions were constantly occupying most of my mental space:

- Did I fully live what was truly meaningful to me?
- Did I do the best I can with all what I have?
- Did I positively impact the world?

I encourage you to look closely into your life. Is your apparent success masking the true answers to these questions and stopping you from getting 100% satisfaction out of life? Are you pursuing outer success at the expense of inner fulfillment?

I have distilled the learnings from my many months in India and years of research into passion and purpose; keep reading and I will help you gain clarity without having to buy a one-way ticket to India!

What does passion mean anyway?

People talk about passion but not many know what it truly means!

Let's start with the dictionary definition of passion:

[pash-uh n] -- which is any powerful or compelling emotion or feeling. It comes from the Latin root-word "passio" which literally means "suffering" or "to endure." Think "Passion of the Christ."

I guess you did not see that coming. People think passion is something that comes to you while on the contrary; passion is that which you are willing to suffer for and endure pleasure and pain in the pursuit of; and in this process you bring passion to life.

So to give you a practical definition of passion that we have distilled from years of helping leaders work and live passionately:

Passion is consistently doing what you love, are good at and is needed by others.

1. *Consistently:* you have to keep it going day-in day-out, passion is not a matter of luck, it's a matter of persistence.
2. *What you love:* you have to be able to do what you love and/or love

what you do, it's a two-way street.
3. *Good at:* as humans we love results and you will never feel good about something you are not good at.
4. *Needed by others:* if your passion has no purpose to serve and does not provide values for others then its just a hobby.

Forget happiness

Happiness is something you give to yourself; it's momentary and superficial. You can be happy eating a chocolate bar or buying a new car and you are bound to feel normal about it once you have it, and then need more and more. This pursuit of happiness is bound to bring you sadness with it. It's impacted by the universal law of polarity: Everything in life has an equal opposite – day and night, male and female, positive and negative, etc., this has been described in Eastern Philosophies as the Yin & Yang.

So if pursuing happiness is not "it" then what should we be looking for?

Fulfillment is the higher level of satisfaction we should be looking for – look at the structure of the word "ful.fill" which simply means to fill-full that of which you have a calling for!

The question then becomes how do we get fulfillment?

Our fulfillment in life is proportional to how much we honor our innermost calling.

Fulfillment is not a question of "either/or" I'm either getting outer happiness or serving a bigger purpose, it's a matter of "and" – I fulfill my calling thus I become fulfilled in life.

The pursuit of happiness and meaning is short when we realize that they can be found when we love what we do and show it.
~ Dr. Marshall Goldsmith

Passion is not only waving your hands

Very relaxed and non-expressive people can be very passionate; cultural differences and styles come into play here. It's very important that you decipher what passion means to you; it's not only about waving your hands and it's not only emotions. Passion comes from the heart and not only how it's expressed physically, it's about how you live your life.

Passion is service

Your passion is a gift from God, you are meant to do it and you are not doing yourself a favor if you are not using it to be of service to the world. Your passion is your participation in this world; it's been given to you to bring to life just like a bird singing or a tree giving fruit and shade.

All of us are born to serve each other and a bigger purpose,
why else are we here!
~ Ron Kaufman

Wrong kind of passion can hurt the world

The quality of your purpose defines the quality of your passion. One can be passionate about the wrong things as well; extreme dictators had passion and terrorists have passion but it's the wrong kind of passion.

If passion drives you, let reason hold the reins.
~ Benjamin Franklin

WHY PURSUE PASSION!

Aside from the thousands of hours I spent researching and studying the topic of passion, I host a talk show called "Passion Sundays" where I have interviewed over 50 global leaders, sports champions, award-winning artists and celebrities diving deep into their interpretation of passion and its impact on all aspects of success and one thing is blazingly obvious: Passion is a crucial element on the journey to success.

Pursuing your passion will put you on the road to becoming everything you are capable of becoming; it puts you in a place of power against all the odds for many reasons:

1- Passion is energy

If you are doing what you love, it provides you with a continuous source of energy that gives you momentum that feeds your willpower. This is one of the most crucial elements to success, because it's not the odds that kill us, but losing the will to fight.

When you are working towards your passion, you will feel fulfilled regardless of the ups and downs and you will have an unlimited source of energy.

Without passion you'll run out of energy long before
your actions yield the desired result.
~ Entrepreneur Magazine

2- Passion brings joyful competitive advantage

In today's highly competitive landscape, it's tough to stay on track if you do not truly love what you do. When you become one with what you do, you are no longer "working" and you will make it very hard for anyone else to compete with you; after all, they are laboring while you are enjoying; the odds become stacked in your favor!

When you feel fulfilled with what you're doing, you don't even call it work, you call it fun!

It's kind of fun to do the impossible.
~ Walt Disney

3- Passion enhances performance

It's simple, when you love something you find ways to make it happen. Where there's a will, there's a way.

This also applies to organizations, as by cultivating the traits of worker passion in their workforce, they can make sustained performance gains and develop the agility needed to outperform competition.

4- Pursuing passion increases clarity

Brian Tracy talks about the key principles of leadership and success that have been discovered in more than 3300 studies going back to 600 BC, and the first one is the principle of "objective" which requires that you are absolutely clear about who you are, what you want, where you are and where you are going. The principle of objective means that you have absolute clarity on what it is you are here on this planet to accomplish.

i. Clarity means focus

When you know what it is exactly that gives you fulfillment in life, you can focus all your efforts on pursuing it. Laser sharp focus is the key to success because then you are bound to find a way to achieve it. When you are that focused, success is no longer a question of "if" it's just a question of "when". It's that kind of focused energy that creates a laser beam capable of cutting the hardest diamonds and so it shapes your life.

ii. Clarity means better decision making

With today's information overload, it's increasingly overwhelming to make decisions; being decisive when required is the difference between success and failure. When you are clear on what you are passionate about, it becomes easier to make timely and effective decisions, which also saves you time and energy, and your probabilities of success increase.

3 STEPS TO LIVE PASSIONATELY!

1. Answer the billion-dollar question...what makes you tick?

Here is one of the most effective and efficient ways to find your passion without having to buy a one-way ticket to India:

Grab your checkbook, write a current dated check to yourself and in the "number" space write $1,000,000,000 and in the "letters" space spell it out: one billion dollars. Go ahead and sign that check.

Look at that check with one billion dollars in your name, tear it off and look at it again – it feels amazing! Feel free to fold it and put it in your pocket, close to your heart.

Now that money is out of the equation, you've got no more financial concerns. Your loved ones are taken care of and you've got enough financial resources to make any dream come true, the question is:

What do you want to do with your life? Would you still be doing what you are doing now?

I know some might say: I will go on a very long holiday, and that's fine, but what's next? As humans we are designed to be productive, so you will get bored after a while. How do you want to invest your time? How do you want to use your energy? What skills do you want learn? What impact do you want to leave on this planet?

Once money is no object and you exit the rat race, what makes you tick?

Be honest with yourself and dare to answer these questions with guts, after all you do have a billion dollars!

Keep in mind in many cases you will start doing something, and after a while you will realize that there are parts of it you enjoy and others that you don't. This is a guide to where you should focus your energy and course correct; living passionately is a journey not a destination.

2. When low on motivation, say "It's Showtime."

On the journey to success you will hit failure after failure and it is normal to occasionally run low on energy and motivation. It's a game of ebb and flow and if you stay close to the vibrancy of your inner core and be true to your values then you will make it through.

In the same way an actor in a Broadway play has to find it in them every day to say, "It's Showtime", a great leader wakes up every morning knowing that the show must go on regardless of how they feel; they are in control of their feelings. Imagine a president waking up in the morning and saying I don't feel like running the country today! Anyone can have passion when times are good; **it's when times are tough that great leaders stand out.**

If you are unable to find external motivation, then tap into your internal inspiration, your "Why" the billion-dollar question! If you answered it from the heart, then you will always find energy there.

If the "Why" is big enough, the "How" takes care of itself.
~ Dr. John Demartini

3. Do your best

You will only be passionate about something you have earned; it's your work that gives value to things and makes you passionate about them. Passion comes from doing your best; it comes as a result of something you keep working hard on till you get good at it.

Your life only gets better when you get better.
~ Brian Tracy

Passion is the most amazing way of living life. This chapter is summarized from our experience in empowering leaders to win the game of work and business of life. It's a great tool to bring out the best in ourselves and the best from each other, hope you found it valuable and practical.

Live Passionately!

About Moustafa

Moustafa Hamwi is known globally as The Passion Guy, he is the founder of Passion Sundays, the world's leading passion and happiness talk show.

Moustafa has interviewed over 50 global leaders, sports champions, award winning artists and celebrities – diving deep into their interpretation of passion and its impact on all aspects of success in business and life, including: leadership, innovation, employee engagement, performance and quality of life. The interview list includes Dr. Marshall Goldsmith, Brian Tracy, Tony Buzan, Ron Kaufman and senior executives from the likes of Google and Microsoft, amongst many others.

Moustafa uses this first of its kind world-class knowledge to deliver powerful insights and global best practices enabling leaders, organizations and government agencies to gain a sustainable advantage through passion and happiness.

Find out how Moustafa can help you ignite passion and win the game of work and business of life on:
- MoustafaHamwi.com
- PassionSundays.com

CHAPTER 10

LIFESTYLE OF A PASSIVE VS. AN ACTIVE INCOME EARNER

BY OTTO BALOGH

MAGYAREGREGY, HUNGARY
February 24, 2003, 6 a.m.

I hated getting up early, but I still did it. If I didn't chop wood and get the fire going, my apartment would be ice cold at two in the afternoon, when I returned from the school where I taught geography.

Once the fire was well-stocked, I dragged my old red bicycle to the street to begin my daily commute. The Russian-made bike had been discarded by one of my students, but it was still usable. There were times, on my way to the Magyaregregy school, that I thought about the hypocrisy of teaching the ten pupils in my class about continents I had never visited.

THE HIGHWAY RETURNING FROM A SAILING TRIP FROM THE
DALMATIAN ISLANDS
September 12, 2009, 10 a.m.

I wanted to sleep. My passenger, the captain of the yacht, jumped at the opportunity to drive the black Lexus, the biggest and newest model of this make. It was several years ahead of its time.

I set the shiatsu massager built into the back seat to level 2, ready to relax. Then it hit me: this had been my 40th vacation in the same number of months. I smiled. "That's probably why I'm so sleepy!"

Hemingway's favorite bar in Cuba . . . Victoria Falls, with the largest circular rainbow of the world . . . the nightclub scene at the 1 Oak in Manhattan with the most notorious partiers of America . . . the raw, wild scent of Africa—no, it was the smell at the Ngorongoro Crater . . . the cafeteria lunch that had cost a dollar with the students in Magyaregregy—no, no, that was before! . . . seeing the world record of Usain Bolt live at the Olympic Games . . . standing at the urinal beside Ronaldinho in the men's room of the VIP section of the China Doll Club . . . the whitewater rafting tour in the Grand Canyon . . . teaching ten thousands of people in Los Angeles about lifestyle. . .

And how many other things!

Well, you can do a lot in 40 months if you have the money. But how is it possible to continuously live the *carpe diem* lifestyle without depleting your financial resources?

I closed my eyes with a smile on my face, because I knew the answer. I figured I'd write a book about it one day. But not now. Now I was going to take a nap.

Written on the island of Koh Samui in a private villa above the water. Beneath the glass floor there are fish. This is important. (...)

How was it possible in just a few years to achieve such a lifestyle shift?

In my book titled *Escape Plan,* I have explained this in details, but if I were to summarize it in three main points those would be as follows:

- I have investigated all four lifestyle quadrants and their deep psychology.
- I have defined in which quadrant I was at each stage in my life, and ESPECIALLY where I am presently.
- I have made the right decisions so I could progress step by step, (quadrant by quadrant), and in particular: by building from the inside out (identity-action plan-implementation) to reach the most ideal quadrant.

And that was the ++ quadrant, the quadrant of financial independence, the freedom I always dreamed of. The childhood dreams have taken over the main role: the travels, the expeditions I have read about in Jules Verne's, Jack London's and Ernest Hemingway's novels. I loved soccer and fishing? I bought a professional indoor soccer team and a private lake. Was I fascinated by the world of the Iditarod and Alaska sled dog racing? I have signed a contract with sled dog racing today's MVP, Dallas Seavey, and under his mentorship I can be at the start line of the 2017 Iditarod as the first Hungarian ... Next adventure? Yes, I have already outlined in my mind a plan for a Guinness record, which will not only require courage, but also time and money ...

But let us see briefly what these four quadrants are?

Our lifestyle - of course besides the fundamental health condition - is influenced mostly by money and leisure time. A combination of these creates the 4 quadrants:

1. −+ (no money, yes time) typically children, retirees, and the unemployed belong to this group. Everyone had such a stage in their lives. This is the Junior Varsity (JV) League of lifestyles.
2. −− (no money, no time) low-income employees, and start up entrepreneurs who invested all of their money and most of their time belong to this group. This should be a temporary lifestyle stage, but many people get stuck until the end of their lives or until the beginning of their retirement. (College League.)
3. +− (lots of money, no time) celebrated by many as the luxury quadrant, but far from the peak. In this stage we can find senior managers or successful entrepreneurs. Their biggest challenge is that, although money can buy them anything, they do not have time to enjoy it, and at a later stage this can cause distress and health issues. (Minor League.)
4. ++ (lots of money and lots of time at the same time). This is the stage where the entrepreneur reaches a level where even without putting in any effort he/she has a constant income (the cash flow coming in). He/she has the money and the time for the people / things / activities that he/she is passionate about. (Major League.) The secret of the ++ lifestyle is the deep understanding and creation of passive income.

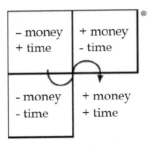

There are two types of income: active and passive. The active income means you are working over and over again, like carrying the drinking water with a bucket from the end of the street to your home. The passive income is built once, and after that the flow just keeps on coming, i.e., like laying down the water pipes, a simple task, but then it is enough to open the valve and flow is coming. Let's see an example of how different two people's lives can be, both of whom make $3,000, but from different income sources.

Imagine that there are two neighbors, both living on $3,000 per month. One of them has an active income, the other a passive one, but financially they live on the same level. Let's see how much their lifestyles differ.

Mr. Active Income gets up at six in the morning. It is a wonderful thing to wake up with the sun—it's what yogis do . . . although they don't grumble while their coffee is brewing. Mr. Active Income, however, has to be at work by eight, so he becomes very upset in the traffic jam; pushy drivers and tailgaters affect his mood. Then he remembers that his boss won't be too happy if he's late, plus he's behind on a project. At his workplace his eyes are on the clock. At five o'clock he's ready to leave, but his boss reminds him that the project has to be completed by the deadline, so he stays for another hour. After he wrestles through the evening rush hour, it's already seven o'clock; by the time he takes a shower and eats his dinner, it's already eight. Another day has passed. Now he sits down to watch TV or goes online to find something worth watching or find something to do on the weekend—the weekend that seems so distant right now.

In the meantime, Mr. Passive Income gets up at half past eight, because this is when his biological clock wakes him up. He doesn't have a private jet either, but he is free to decide what to do today: he loves painting, so he spends half a day in his private studio. Then he is ready to play tennis. He knows that exercise is important, and although he isn't an all-day-workout guy, he enjoys tennis. He owns five condos, all of them are rented out, and one of his tenants is a young student who not only is a good conversationalist but also was a tennis champion in high school, and he can learn a lot from him. After tennis he decides to surprise his children and picks them up after school, then takes them out for ice cream. That evening he has an appointment to meet somebody to discuss an additional source of passive income. If everything goes according to his plans, his passive monthly income will reach $10,000 in two years, and then he will be able to realize his dream, which is to spend two months in Tahiti every year. Gauguin is his role model, so he wants to paint there.

The same amount of money, but what a difference in lifestyle and in prospects! This is the difference between the active and the passive income.

Now let's jump forward in time.

Two years later, professionally, the luckiest possible thing happens to Mr. Active Income, and in the shortest possible time. He is not only promoted, but due to a favorable interplay of circumstances and, of course, thanks to his professional expertise, he is appointed assistant manager of the subsidiary of his company. His active income has increased more than three-fold, from $3,000 to $10,000 each month—a great source of happiness and pride!

But now he has to be in the office even earlier. He can't just show up at one minute to eight. On one hand, he has to set a good example for the employees, and on the other hand, his superior would certainly dislike it if he slacked off right after his promotion. His working hours no longer end at five or even six: now he has to take some work home in the evenings and over the weekends. He must keep his cell phone with him at all times and has to answer any calls about work—it's in his contract.

He carries a huge amount of responsibility on his shoulders, and he feels a cold knot in his stomach and hot perspiration on his palms each time he has to make a decision. Make just one or two mistakes, and the hyenas are already there to take his place. He usually skips lunch, and he no longer sleeps so peacefully at night. He manages an ice-cream factory with nationwide distribution, and lately he is being blamed even for the weather not being hot enough. His thoughts before falling asleep are a hope that there will be sweltering heat tomorrow.

By this time, Mr. Passive Income has also achieved his goal: his passive income has increased from $3,000 each month to $10,000. The two years that went by didn't wear him down; he actually looks younger by a few years. His skin and his face, but especially his eyes, all look younger. He only remarks with a small smile: "I challenged the ravages of time and they decided to bypass me." He has been in Tahiti for the past few weeks, staying in a luxurious villa hidden in the jungle, where he paints to his heart's content; he doesn't even eat on some days, just munches on fruit.

On other days he doesn't want to see his paintbrushes and instead goes fishing. In the evening he enjoys time in the villa with some good wine. Gauguin left everything and everybody behind, believing that from isolation came the artist's genius, but Mr. Passive Income is at peace with the idea that he won't achieve worldwide fame. He doesn't even feel that this should be his goal. Perhaps in another life. What he really wants is to get closer to nature and through this to his own soul—this is his ultimate goal now. It's a fascinating journey: the deeper he goes, the more extraordinary the colors are. Earlier, he only suspected that it was possible to find so much enjoyment in the silence, the colors, and even the pulsing heat at noon. Will he go home in a few weeks when the month is over? He doesn't know. He has come to enjoy living in the present. He will decide then and there.

A (probable) remark by the reader: "This is all very nice, but it's only possible in fairy tales." I disagree. If you find the right means to generate passive income, it can become very real, and you can get there in a relatively short time. I managed to build a passive income equivalent to the rent from 30 apartments. It took me 20 months, starting not with five, but from scratch, and I am far from holding a record in this field. But decision is first, the how is coming second.

About Otto

Otto is a teacher, networker, starter-upper, writer, extreme athlete, coach.

Otto was born in the communist Romania, from Hungarian parents. After graduation, he rejected several job offers and hitchhiked to Hungary: first he lived off of casual work, then started purposefully building his career. At a young age, it became apparent to him that the development of people and teams were of the greatest interest to him. He finds credibility of the utmost importance: Teaching success should be done by those who have a proven track record of success.

The building blocks of his personal philosophy are:

- Coming from behind the victory is always sweeter.
- What doesn't kill you, makes you stronger.
- The last will be first.
- It is never too late to live your dreams.

He learns to ride a bike at the age of 13, at the age of 28 he learns to drive a car and learns to swim at the age of 31, but when he turns 32, he makes his first $1M, and even though he has never been an athlete in any sports, he qualifies at the age of 39 for the famous Iditarod sled dog race held in Alaska – which is considered as being the world's toughest race.

He teaches the same financial independence while writing and making public appearances, and as an example, he travels 90 times one week each month to more than 50 countries.

As an independent partner of NuSkin Enterprises, he builds a network in 30 countries with teams reaching hundreds of thousands of members in the past decade. He manages more than $100M worth of products (vitamins and cosmetics). He builds an educational/leadership system, the System7, which now has been adopted in five continents. He is a sought-after motivational speaker in three languages, and has presented for audiences from Jakarta, Paris, Los Angeles, etc.

His publications, focused around the two topics of Success and Financial Independence, have sold hundreds of thousands of copies around the globe. He wrote three books, two for professional/internal use and one dedicated to the wide public. The latter, *Escape Plan*, has been translated into six languages, including English! It also became one of the best-selling motivational books in Hungary.

Currently, he supports several innovative startups and administers several blogs.

His charity portfolio encompasses his regions burning problems, but also has been supporting Africa's starving children every month for more than 10 years.

With his personal life examples, his books, and his personal consulting seminars, his objective is maximizing human potential. He is particularly interested in the mission, potential, human relations, leadership topics, and considers that life is nothing but a research expedition, meant to map these topics. His personal mission is finding a solution to the human self-limiting patterns and beliefs.

Otto is now 40 years old, living in Budapest and in Alaska. His summer season is spent in Europe and during the winter season he is preparing with his dog team to compete and successfully finish the Iditarod.

For more details about passive income, ++ lifestyle and Financial Freedom in his book titled, *Escape Plan*, and/or to connect with him through his Facebook page:
- www.facebook.com/ottobaloghofficial

CHAPTER 11

GIFT THE GENERATIONAL INTEREST FASHIONING TRANSFER TRUST (GIFTT®)

– AN AVANT-GARDE METHOD OF TRANSFERRING WEALTH, TAX-SHELTERED, WHILE KEEPING IT ASSET-PROTECTED DURING YOUR LIFETIME.

BY WALLACE R. ("WALLY") NICHOLS, JD, MBA

What if you had a highly appreciated asset, perhaps a beach house, or a business, or a group of investments, that you wanted to continue to enjoy the benefits of, while simultaneously asset protecting from creditors and predators, continue to control, but yet pass on at tax-advantaged values to your next generation of beneficiaries? This technique may be as close to having your cake and eating it too as we can legally get in the United States. Always remember, just like insurance, when you have to buy it when you don't need it, you have to protect assets from creditors *before* a claim arises. That's why we call it estate *planning*, and specifically here, why we call this a special "GIFTT®" planning technique—because it's a proactive process, not a reactive one!

The GIFTT planning approach helps minimize the family's wealth transfer costs yet simultaneously keeps flexibility, and perhaps best of all, retains control over assets as needed and desired. We call it Generational because, most frequently, we use multiple family generations in both the creation, funding, control, and passing on of the trust assets ("trust corpus").

We use the term "Interest" as a double-entendre to refer to both the "interests" of each generation (and party to the trust) involved in this type of planning, as well as the "interest" paid to you (as our client and primary beneficiary) through the promissory note, or loan, we will have the trust owe you. We use the strange term in this instance, "Fashioning" – because we are shaping, creating, and transforming highly appreciated assets from you into a form whereby such assets will be asset protected, and passed on to your next-generation beneficiaries at tax-advantaged values via a trust created for your benefit by your parents (usually), a generation preceding you. Finally, we use the nomenclature, "Transfer" and "Trust" for obvious reasons.

Estate planning, asset protection planning, wealth transfer attorneys use a variety of techniques and legal mechanisms to accomplish their clients' stated goals. Most frequently such goals are asset protection, probate avoidance, and minimizing federal and state tax implications. Included in these are often the use of gift tax exemptions, income-shifting approaches valuation discounts, installment note sales, creditor protection devices, and tax-shifting approaches.

Trust income shifting and tax-shifting approaches are important to grasp because tax rates increase rapidly on trusts at very low income amounts compared to individual tax rates. So, we like to shift such income tax liability from the trust to an individual who pays lower taxes due to the comparatively lower individual tax rate at the same amounts of income. Now, you understand the concept and desirability of "grantor trust" status! Here, we have made the trust "intentionally defective" in terms of the tax code, so that the individual remains responsible for the income tax even though the individual has given to the trust legal title of the assets. So, it should be easy for you to see why popular estate planning tools such as grantor-retained annuity trusts and intentionally defective grantor trusts offer many benefits. They enable you to leverage valuation discounts to reduce gift, estate, and generation-skipping transfer taxes. And they allow you to freeze asset values at their date of contribution levels, protecting all future appreciation from federal or state transfer taxes. These tools take advantage of the grantor trust rules to generate additional estate planning benefits such as tax savings. Again, the trust income is taxed to you, as grantor, allowing the assets to grow tax-free and preserving more of your wealth for future generations.

Essentially, your tax payments are additional, tax-free gifts to your children, or other beneficiaries. Because a grantor trust is your alter ego, you can sell its appreciated assets, thereby removing them from your estate, with no income tax consequences. Yet, despite these benefits, most traditional trusts suffer from a significant disadvantage: the loss of control. That is, you must relinquish the right to control, use, or direct the ultimate disposition of, the trust assets. If you wish to take advantage of trust estate planning techniques but you're not ready to let go of your wealth, a new cutting-edge type of trust may be a viable solution for your situation: the "Generational Interest Fashioning Transfer Trust," (GIFTT®).

There have not been any published litigation or court opinions testing this method of planning to date that this author has been able to find in any jurisdiction of the United States. But, the IRS has issued private letter rulings ("PLRs") which certainly do not rule out the use of the GIFTT, or similarly designed trust planning techniques. Moreover, and in fact, these IRS PLRs appear to support the idea of the GIFTT. Still, it is important to remember while we are discussing this technique, that PLRs do not constitute legal precedent and may only be formally relied upon by the taxpayer for whom the ruling was issued.

I. What's a GIFTT®?

Fundamentally, a GIFTT is a trust established by someone *other than* the person who is the lawyer's client (we will refer to that person as a "third party"). The GIFTT is **designed to give the client control** as an investment trustee and **beneficial enjoyment** as a primary beneficiary **of the trust property in the GIFTT® (the "corpus")**. This way the client can use and manage the trust assets without compromising the trust's ability to avoid transfer taxes at the client's death.

Secondly, the GIFTT® protects trust assets from the client's creditors during the client's life. At the client's death, control of the trust passes to the client's descendants, subject to the client's ability to change the disposition of the trust assets through the exercise of a special power of appointment. Remember, the client was the trust's primary beneficiary. So, in addition to receiving control of the trust, the subsequent primary beneficiaries also may receive benefits of trust-owned properties, such as the transfer tax avoidance, and creditor protection, the latter of which includes protection from a divorcing or separated spouse. What a powerful concept!

II. Too Good to Be True?

Now, the skeptical among you will immediately begin to question how keeping control of assets while simultaneously protecting those assets from creditors could possibly work. After all, there is no free lunch, and creditor protection is generally a function of layering assets akin to the layers of an onion, the peeling off of which brings tears to the creditors' eyes. Well, that's all true. But what is also true is the ancient principal that assets received by gift or inheritance from a third-party, which assets are retained in a properly structured trust, are protected from unnecessary exposure to taxing authorities and the beneficiary's creditors. Moreover, such creditors include judgment creditors, a divorcing spouse, an unhappy family member, or a disgruntled business partner. While IRS rules prohibit you from transferring assets to beneficiaries on a tax-advantaged basis if you retain the right to use or control those assets, those rules do not apply to assets you *receive from others* in a beneficiary controlled trust. The challenge in taking advantage of the GIFTT is to *place assets you currently own into a third-party trust.* So, let's take a closer look at the features the GIFTT® offers.

III. Advantages and Nuances of the GIFTT®

First, the Beneficiary enjoys access to trust assets and appreciation of those assets without causing estate tax inclusion. So long as the Beneficiary has not made any gifts to the trust or transferred assets for less than the fair and adequate consideration of those assets ("fair market value" or "FMV"), trust assets should not be included in the Beneficiary's taxable estate.

Secondly, the Beneficiary can serve as a trustee and thus can control investment and management decisions with respect to trust assets. Just remember that the Beneficiary can have no control over decisions with respect to any life insurance owned by the GIFTT® on the Beneficiary's life and in that instance, should not serve as sole trustee. It's always better that the Beneficiary serve as co-trustee along with an independent trustee in those circumstances.

The Beneficiary can have a special power of appointment to change the ultimate beneficiaries of the trust without causing estate tax inclusion, not counting insurance on his own life, which should not cause estate tax inclusion because the Beneficiary is not the grantor of the trust.

The Beneficiary pays the trust income taxes, thereby preserving more of the trust assets for wealth transfer purposes. Effectively, when the Beneficiary pays the trust's income taxes, such are considered a tax-free transfer from the Beneficiary to the trust.

Ostensibly because of the alter-ego status between the Beneficiary and the GIFTT® for IRS purposes, the Beneficiary recognizes no gains on the sale of assets to the GIFTT® and the interest payments received on an installment note are not income taxable to the Beneficiary. Again, assets sold by the Beneficiary to the GIFTT® may be protected from the reach of the Beneficiary's creditors and can appreciate outside the Beneficiary's taxable estate.

IV. GIFTT® Example

Let's look at an example. First a parent or other third-party creates an irrevocable trust and contributes $5000 in cash naming you, my client, as the Beneficiary. No other gifts are made to the trust by anyone. The trust creator is the grantor of the trust for transfer tax purposes, creditor rights purposes, but not income tax purposes. The GIFTT® is an irrevocable, fully discretionary, generation-skipping tax exempt trust. The Beneficiary is given a limited-time power to withdraw the original gift (the *Crummey* power) after which such time expires the *Crummey* power expires or lapses. After that happens, the Beneficiary is the "owner" of the trust for income tax purposes. This is because the original Beneficiary is taxed on trust income. Accordingly, the Beneficiary's estate will have already paid the taxes on trust income by the time of the Beneficiary's death. This effectively shifts the Beneficiary's personal wealth transfer tax free into the GIFTT® and away from creditors. Such shift is without gift or GST tax consequences and with no economic risk (as to the Beneficiary) because the Beneficiary is in control of trust investments.

Creation of the Trust

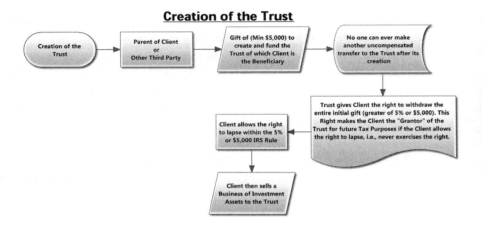

V. Sale of Business or Investment Assets

The purpose of this GIFTT® is for the sale of business or investment assets. After the Crummey right of withdrawal has lapsed, the Beneficiary sells to the trust business or investment assets in exchange for a secured promissory note with interest paid or accrued at the applicable federal rate ("AFR"). The sale will be of a defined value and a gift tax return would be filed reporting the transaction as a non-gift. That's a Gift Tax Form 709 disclosure. The promissory note will be secured by the GIFTT® by paying a guarantee fee to the guarantors of the note. Guarantors of the note could be an existing irrevocable trust, the Beneficiary spouse, the creator of the trust, or any other party who has sufficient assets to satisfy the guarantee if necessary.

Now, the Beneficiary holds a promissory note in the amount of the value of the assets sold to the GIFTT. The GIFTT® owns the initial gift of $5000 and the business or investment assets it just purchased from the Beneficiary. The guarantors, in exchange for a guarantee fee paid to them annually by the GIFTT®, now owe the GIFTT® the obligation of a partial guarantee of the promissory note.

Client Sale of Assets to Trust and Purchase of Life Insurance

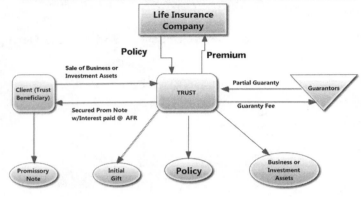

VI. Annual Administration

The GIFTT® receives income from the business or investment assets and other assets it holds. The GIFTT® pays the annual interest and any principal prepayment on the promissory note to the Beneficiary. That payment is disregarded for income tax purposes by the GIFTT®. Further, all income on trust assets are taxed to the Beneficiary and the payment of that income tax by the Beneficiary on the trust income is not a gift to the GIFTT® for gift tax purposes. The GIFTT® also pays a continuing guarantee fee to the guarantors of the promissory note.

Annual Administration of Sale of Business or Investment Assets

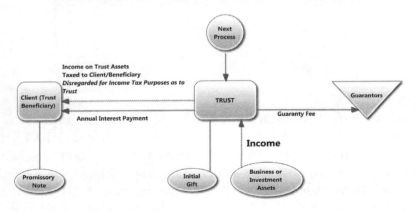

VII. *The Promissory Note Balloon Payment Becomes Due, is Paid, and thus is Extinguished.*

Completion of Sale At End of Note Term

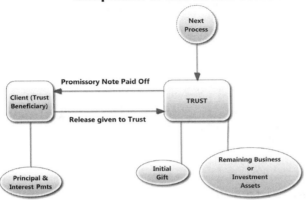

Upon fully repaying the loan balance at the end of the promissory note's term, the Beneficiary gives a satisfaction and release from the promissory note to the GIFTT®. The income on GIFTT® assets continues to be taxed to the Beneficiary for life and the GIFTT® continues to pay that income to the Beneficiary for life.

Following Client's Death

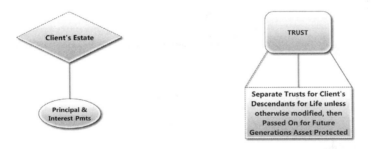

At the Beneficiary's death, the Beneficiary's estate now owns all the principal, interest and income received from the GIFTT®. The GIFTT® then creates separate dynasty trusts for each descendent of the Beneficiary for life, which are then recycled down for future generations, absent modification by the exercise of a limited power appointment. Note that these separate trusts are protected from the descendants' creditors, spouses and the generation-skipping transfer tax for their lives.

VIII. Another Example: Sale of Business/Investment Assets, Plus Purchase of Life Insurance

Now let's look at a second example of adding a life insurance policy on the Beneficiary. We begin with the same initial creation of the GIFTT® just as before. And, just as before, the Beneficiary sells business assets or investment assets to the GIFTT® in exchange for a secured promissory note with interest paid or accrued at the AFR. This time however, the GIFTT® purchases life insurance on the Beneficiary's life.

Client Sale of Assets to Trust and Purchase of Life Insurance

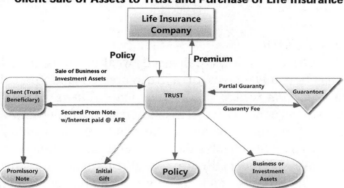

The GIFTT® makes the initial premium on the policy. The GIFTT® is the owner of the life insurance policy. If the GIFTT® did not generate enough cash flow to pay those premiums, the Beneficiary could enter into a private premium financing arrangement with the GIFTT® to ensure those premiums were paid. Remember, the Beneficiary cannot hold trustee powers over the insurance on the Beneficiary's life and the Beneficiary cannot hold a power of appointment over that policy.

Annual administration of the GIFTT® continues as in the previous example. This time at the Beneficiary's death, however, the life insurance company pays death benefits into the GIFTT® thereby enhancing the value passed on by the GIFTT® to the Beneficiary's descendants into their separate Dynasty trusts.

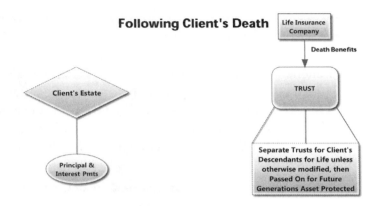

IX. CONCLUSION

The GIFTT® allows enhanced wealth, transfer tax, and asset protection advantages of a trust created and funded by a third party *for the benefit of the Beneficiary/client.* The GIFTT® offers investment control of trust assets and access to and enjoyment of trust property by the Beneficiary/client (who is the primary Beneficiary of the trust). So, clients otherwise reluctant to comprehensively plan, or make significant lifetime wealth transfers for others, can now enjoy the benefits of advanced wealth and asset protection planning for themselves with minimal personal, financial, and tax risk.

About Wally

Wallace R. Nichols, JD, MBA is the President of W.R. Nichols Law. Wallace R. Nichols is a distinguished attorney based in Atlanta, Georgia with offices also in Phoenix, Arizona. His firm, W.R. Nichols Law, focuses on strategic wealth transfer planning so clients of all ages keep and protect themselves and their descendants from creditors and predators. These strategies range from entrepreneurial protection, to Children's Protection Planning for young families, to Estate Planning and Strategic Wealth Transfers for middle-aged folks, to end-of-life and long-term care planning for Elders. Nichols designs strategies to preserve wealth, protect from claims, or help Elders qualify for VA Pension Planning or Medicaid while still providing for a family legacy.

As he tells it, Nichols' decision to go into law was a natural one. . .

"I decided to become a lawyer when I was nine years old. That year, 1968, was a horrifically bloody year. My brother had just survived the bloodiest Thet Offensive of the Viet Nam war. I was hospitalized with scarlet fever the night Dr. Martin Luther King, Jr., was assassinated in Memphis, TN. I relapsed into nephritis when Senator Robert F. Kennedy was assassinated in Los Angeles, CA. The Democratic National Convention in Chicago later that year was fraught with protest, riots, and blood. Then, on Christmas Eve 1968 the first men orbited the moon and we saw this lonely blue marble floating in blackness of space. I realized that courage and leadership in the face of cowardice and bloody retaliation could bring needed change. But, fundamental change occurs through the legal system. So, I decided I would become a lawyer."

Nichols' trial experience includes trust and probate issues, fraud and fiduciary litigation, Elder Law issues, and select civil rights cases.

Also a licensed financial advisor, Nichols advises clients on a wide range of financial investment choices to complement their legal estate planning, utilizing his financial planning firm, Asset Guidance Group, LLC. The result: clients see their estate as a holistic blend of interlocking financial and legal elements, experiencing increased privacy by using a single, consummate professional.

"My boutique office addresses the needs of Baby Boomers who are turning 65 years of age at rates exceeding 9,000/day. I design customized strategic decumulation strategies so Boomers do not outlive their money. Longevity driven by rapidly advancing technology is the new pressing challenge of our age. For the first time in American history, two generations of a family can be simultaneously institutionalized in skilled nursing or assisted-living facilities. This happened in my own family, prompting me

to author an introductory book on the topic: Pack a Sweater: Preparing Boomers for Long Term Care."

Detailed Career Information

Wallace R. Nichols received his Juris Doctor from the University of New Mexico School of Law, his M.B.A. from Texas Tech University, and his B.B.A. from Angelo State University. Mr. Nichols is a member of the State Bars of Arizona and Georgia, the District of Columbia Bar, and all courts in those jurisdictions.

CHAPTER 12

MAKING BETTER BUSINESS DECISIONS AS A PRINCIPLED PERFORMER

BY JASON MEFFORD

On the morning of Friday, 18 September 2015, I received an alert on my phone: "The [Environmental Protection Agency] EPA set to make an announcement about a major automaker at 12:00 PM EST today." The gears in my mind started turning at high speed.

At the time, I was a shareholder in a major automaker and wondered how this announcement would affect me as an individual investor. Usually these sorts of announcements, especially from the EPA or another government regulator, were not a good sign for an organization's stock value. It usually meant the organization had done something illegal and was about to be penalized. The news, and the penalty, usually lead to a significant decline in the stock price, at least for the short-term.

Was the company I was invested in the culprit? I monitored my phone closely that day until I heard the news.

The press conference was to announce the EPA issued a Notice of Violation (NOV) to Volkswagen, alleging that four-cylinder Volkswagen and Audi diesel cars from model years 2009-2015 included defeat device software that circumvented EPA emissions standards for certain air pollutants. The NOV alleged Volkswagen loaded a sophisticated software algorithm onto almost 500,000 vehicles in the United States.

This defeat device software could detect when the car was undergoing official emissions testing, turning on controls to pass the test, but under normal driving situations the cars would emit nitrogen oxides up to forty times the standard allowed by law. Such devices, which provide false information about the actual pollutant levels in order to evade the clean air standards, are illegal.

The stock market and I were left to wonder what would this mean for Volkswagen. We all knew this was just the beginning of something much bigger, but how much bigger we did not know. How would this affect Volkswagen's stock price? Over the course of the next few days more information became available.

When the stock market opened on Monday, 21 September 2015, Volkswagen's stock started its decline by dropping almost 20% in one day.

On Tuesday, 22 September 2015, Volkswagen announced there were eleven million vehicles world-wide equipped with the defeat device software, 10.5 million more cars than the US EPA was alleging. They also set aside a provision of $7.3 billion "to cover the necessary service measures and other efforts to win back the trust of our customers."[1] The stock continued to drop.

Over the course of the two weeks following the announcement from the EPA, Volkswagen's stock price plummeted almost 40%. That means, shareholders who invested in Volkswagen lost almost 40% of their wealth due to this particular event and the market's reaction. An event that appears to have started all the way back in 2007 and was the result of a series of bad decisions. Decisions that did not take into account the full impact they would have on the value of Volkswagen.

The example of Volkswagen is become ever more common in the media. This begs the questions of why, what and how. Why are these sorts of events happening to large, sophisticated organizations? What can we learn from them to make sure our organizations don't suffer similar events and losses? How can we make better decisions?

Running an organization is similar to being a juggler. There are several different balls an organization must continually juggle. Organizations have multiple objectives to achieve, but also have to be concerned with uncertainty and business risks they face, while complying with laws, regulations and promises they have made to various stakeholders. The concept of Principled Performance[2], is the reliable achievement of objectives, while addressing uncertainty and acting with integrity. The three "balls" an organization must juggle are:

1) governance or performance
2) risk management
3) compliance

When organizations get into trouble, they effectively "drop" one or two of these balls, usually because they are so focused on the others. Successful organizations do a better job of juggling these three balls, keeping their eye on all three as they fly through the air. Organizations that practice Principled Performance have capabilities in place to ensure all three balls are juggled and monitored to ensure one of them does not get dropped.

Organizations are created to meet specific objectives or identified needs. For many organizations, a major objective is to earn money and make a profit, or return, for its owners and investors.Even public sector (governmental) and non-profit entities are concerned about staying within financial budgets and providing a net contribution, that can be used to provide those public services. Other objectives often relate to strategic, operational, customer objectives, or processes. Sometimes these objectives can compete with each other. For example, the objective of making a profit may take a backseat to increasing sales. Organizations may sacrifice profit by taking a strategy to lower prices to increase the volume of sales.

Regardless of the type of organization, a group of individuals came together seeing some opportunities or needs in the marketplace. For example, an opportunity to make money from providing a new or different product or service; or a need for some public services to help their community. They developed specific objectives and created a business model to meet those objectives. Business models include strategies, processes, technology and infrastructure that help organizations meet their objectives.

Governance or performance relates to how an organization is structured from the owners, board of directors, senior management, management, and on down to the employees. This is how the organization has developed strategies, processes, technology and infrastructure to help achieve its objectives.

Along the road to meeting objectives, uncertainty occurs—uncertainty that invariably has an impact on whether or not the organization will meet its objectives. This uncertainty comes in the form of certain opportunities and threats. This uncertainty creates obstacles the organization must navigate around on the way to meeting its objectives and is the reason for taking a risk management approach to business.

Organizations have to make decisions today about uncertain future events. They have to make decisions affecting investment of money, people, infrastructure and resources, without knowing for sure if the investment will pay off. The process used for making the best decisions possible, based on this uncertainty, is called risk management.

In addition to navigating around the obstacles, an organization must also stay within certain mandatory and voluntary boundaries. Mandatory boundaries include those requirements imposed on an organization by an external party: for example, laws and regulations. Voluntary boundaries are values, policies, procedures, processes, contracts and promises the organization has voluntarily chosen to follow. Often these voluntary promises are made in public statements expressed to its stakeholders, or are in the form of agreements with its business partners.

In order for organizations to exist in today's business environment, they are granted license to do business from a government entity. The legal structures organizations use, such as corporations, partnerships, limited-liability companies, come with certain expectations. The governments where these organizations are domiciled expect the organizations to follow the necessary laws and regulations. Other stakeholders who work with the organization also have expectations, usually in the form of promises and contracts. Maintaining the trust with these stakeholders, by following the laws, regulation, promises and contracts, and, being able to prove this trust, is called compliance.

A stakeholder is a person, group, or organization that has direct or indirect stake in an organization because it can affect or be affected by the organization's actions, objectives, and policies. This is a very broad definition, but in today's inter-connected world, it means almost anyone can be a stakeholder of your organization. Some of the most common stakeholders include: investors, employees, vendors, customers, communities, and government regulators.

The answer to our first question: Why are these sorts of events happening to large, sophisticated organizations? Organizations are dropping one of the three balls. In the case of Volkswagen, it appears decisions were made starting back in 2007 to help them sell cars that weren't designed to meet the new environmental regulations. Including defeat device software on these cars would help them meet their objectives of selling more cars and making more profits, but at the expense of sacrificing compliance with laws and regulations. At the time the decision was made, I surmise someone thought it more important to meet the sales and profit objectives, than to comply with the law. They effectively allowed the compliance ball to come crashing to the ground while they focused on selling more automobiles in their effort to become the largest car company in the world.

What those individuals failed to realize is how the loss of trust, caused by non-compliance, would impact meeting their objectives. This is a common mistake made by managers: not anticipating the full impact our decisions may have on the organization. We already know they have taken a $7.3 billion write-off, and several experts are anticipating this event will cost Volkswagen at least $30 billion. The loss of trust has led to a significant decrease in sales in the 4th quarter of 2015, and the potential for lawsuits from various stakeholder groups.

In business school, I was taught, like many other business students, that our key objective as managers of an organization was to "maximize shareholder value." I don't think that is an incorrect statement, but I believe many business managers misinterpret short-term profits as the key to shareholder value. Shareholder value is a long-term principle, and as we have seen with the Volkswagen example, shareholder value can be erased very quickly by dropping one of the balls. Managers need to be more concerned about what is right for the organization in the long-term, not the next quarterly earnings release, or even next year's revenues.

It can take years for someone to notice when a ball drops. We see in the case of Volkswagen, and others, like the penalties assessed on the US banks related to the sub-prime mortgage issue from 2008, when it is the compliance ball that drops, the government will eventually come knocking at the door demanding justice. In both of these examples it took the government seven or eight years before sanctions and penalties were assessed, erasing much of the prior profits.

The answer to our second question: What can we learn from them to make sure our organizations don't suffer similar events and losses? Organizations need to take a more Principled Performance approach to business, considering and integrating governance, risk management, and compliance processes to ensure the balls don't drop. In large, complex organizations these functions are usually managed by different people who often do not communicate. Developing capabilities to ensure the organization makes decisions in a Principled Performance manner, considering the impact decisions have on governance, risk management and compliance, will help ensure one or more of the balls don't get dropped.

So, how can we make better decisions? We can develop capabilities and decision-making models to help our managers make decisions that consider all three balls: governance, risk management and compliance. We can use frameworks and models, such as the OCEG GRC[3] Capability Model (www.oceg.org) to help us ensure we have the necessary components and elements built into our capabilities to ensure our managers are making decisions that consider the governance, risk management and compliance aspects of our business. We can encourage communication between the various functions in our organization that impact these three areas. We can develop decision-making models to help ensure our managers consider all of the impacts their decisions have on the organization, in the short-term and the long-term. We can align our performance, compensation, and incentive programs in such a way to ensure we encourage our managers to be vigilant in juggling all three balls, without damaging our reputation or failing to anticipate a risk.

In short, we can make better business decisions when we consider the concept of Principled Performance. We have to think: How can I reliably achieve my objectives, while addressing uncertainty and acting with integrity? What is the decision that will allow me to achieve my objectives, manage the uncertainties and risks I face, but doesn't sacrifice my integrity?

If we don't make decisions considering all three areas in a principled way, we will find ourselves just like Volkswagen, and countless others, giving back more than a short-term gain when a ball drops.

Endnotes

1. http://www.volkswagenag.com/content/vwcorp/info_center/en/news/2015/09/Volkswagen_AG_has_issued_the_following_information.html
2. The term Principled Performance is a trademark of OCEG, used with permission (www.oceg.org).
3. OCEG GRC: Open Compliance and Ethics Group - Governance, Risk Management & Compliance

About Jason

Jason Mefford is a sought-after speaker, business trainer and coach on ethics, corporate governance, risk management, GRC, compliance and internal audit topics. He helps organizations think differently by becoming Principled Performers to help them reliably achieve their objectives, while addressing uncertainty and acting with integrity. He is currently the President of Mefford Associates, a professional training, coaching and boutique advisory firm, and is also a Brian Tracy certified trainer and business coach.

Jason has spent many years training and coaching top business professionals all over the world, and is consistently rated as one of the leading experts and most effective speakers and trainers in the world. He is the author of *Risk-Based Internal Auditing,* and was a contributing author on the OCEG GRC Capability Model v3.0.

He is a Fellow with the Open Compliance and Ethics Group (OCEG), a nonprofit think tank that uniquely helps organizations drive Principled Performance® by enhancing corporate culture and integrating governance, risk management, and compliance processes. The concept of Principled Performance® allows organizations to reliably achieve their objectives, while addressing uncertainty and acting with integrity - the principles necessary for organizations to succeed over the long-term.

He has been recognized by Yale University as a rising star in corporate governance, and was a finalist for the *Corporate Secretary Magazine* rising star in corporate governance award.

Jason is a graduate of Boise State University (BBA in Accountancy) and the University of Southern California's Marshall School of Business (MBA in Business).

You can connect with Jason at:
- Jmefford@meffordassociates.com
- www.twitter.com/JasonLeeMefford
- www.facebook.com/JasonLeeMefford
- https://www.linkedin.com/in/jasonmefford

To learn more, please visit:
- www.jasonmefford.com
- www.meffordassociates.com
- www.meffordmultimedia.com

CHAPTER 13

CREATING THE CURRENT
– HOW A PASSION CAN BECOME YOUR WAY TO PEACE AND FINANCIAL STABILITY

BY ADIYB MUHAMMAD

I guess I will start by saying, I have never been so happy and at peace with my circumstances as I am now. This is due to having the feeling of assurance that my life is going well by the results I see in my chosen passion.

As with a lot of people, there were times in my life that it seemed like I was being constantly bombarded by problem, after problem, after problem; and no matter how hard I worked, I just couldn't get ahead— especially financially. Nor did I feel fulfilled in any job I was doing. They were mostly service jobs, like maintenance, warehouse, and kitchen jobs early on during my high school years. Now I landed a construction job pouring concrete one summer in the 11th grade which I looked at as fine, because I ended up in great shape because of running with a "Georgia" bucket full of concrete and pouring it where I was told in order to build driveways and lots. As a young man of 16, I looked at it as being paid to exercise.

Now my parents weren't particularly well off; and I felt that in order to go to college I had to work or go into the military to get benefits to help with school. I decided to go with the Army. This was actually during the Vietnam conflict in 1972. I was young and I guess you would say somewhat patriotic. First, I enlisted into the National Guard which actually sends you away for individual training in advance for the job you will have in the military. While I was away, I decided to go "regular army" and serve at that time. I initially thought I would be going to Vietnam, but fortunately, President Nixon decided to no longer send men to Viet Nam. So after medical training, I ended up in South Korea and on to an evacuation hospital in Seoul. Okay, after serving about 18 months in Korea, which was a great experience in my opinion, I returned to the States to be stationed at home in DC at Walter Reed Army Medical Center in 1975. I worked on a rotating schedule in the emergency room. I ended my time in service in 1976.

I didn't go to school right away and got a job working at a city government facility that housed DC prisoners in a medical evaluation scenario. The unit was set up to evaluate as to whether a prisoner was competent to stand trial in DC courts. I did shift work from 7 to 3 or 3 to 11, 7 days a week with varying days off. My military training actually helped me to exercise the discipline to do my job; but, I didn't see a real future for myself at that time. I was seriously thinking I was helping people in my capacity in being a nursing assistant to the inmates. A funny thing happened while I was working there, some of the people I met were family members of folks that I knew growing up in DC. So, the job became personal for me. I became acutely aware of the care the inmates were receiving at the unit. The one question I asked at the time: *"How can we evaluate them fairly if we keep them on medication constantly?"*

The "powers that be" – meaning the unit administrator – felt that I was insubordinate for asking the question. Being around 21 at the time, I thought it was a legitimate question. Thus, I learned a lesson – you should know your environment and your environment's culture, questioning individuals in a more acceptable way. I believe the way I presented the question insinuated that they were not doing a good job. This was as opposed to presenting the question with a possible solution or an alternative—just my thoughts. Needless to say, when I began questioning the way the unit ran, I seemed to be ostracized for being a troublemaker which made me uncomfortable, and as a young man that saw no future there, I left and got another job.

Shortly after, I found another opportunity working as a Regional

Coordinator for a youth program. Now, about 22 years old, I worked with a multitude of 14 to 21-year-olds with the DC Youth Congress program that taught kids how the City made decisions and how their families were affected; and, how important it was to at least understand the power of the city government agencies. Also, at that time, I was a Political Science major, with a Business minor. I landed a job with the Job Corps as a residential advisor for the youth up to the age of 22. At this time, I was around 23 years old myself, I could relate to the youngsters. I learned a great deal about the struggles of being young through my story and the story of others.

By the way, I had gotten married when I was 20 and around this time my first son was born. The birth of my son made me realize that I wanted and needed more. It always seemed I was reaching for other positions of employment, but never focusing in on what I could accomplish with the jobs I had. I was just thinking if I got a better job it would be the answer to creating a better life.

For months I went to work at my job, then two jobs, in order to make ends meet. I ended up working at a telemarketing job, then two telemarketing jobs. One from 8 to 5 and the other 5:30 to 10. The first job was setting appointments for payroll processing and tax filing services and the second for a heating and air conditioning service. It was these jobs that introduced me to the concept of selling as a viable means to generate income. I realized when I set the appointments and the salesmen closed the sale, this generated a significant income because they were well dressed, drove nice cars and spoke about nice homes. I decided "that's what I needed to be doing."

So basically, my chance came. By working at the heating and air conditioning company, I had friend who knew the manager of a new technology company that was about to go public; he invited me to come and interview. At the time I didn't know anything about technology. When I went to the interview, the interview went well from the stand point the intent was the company was setting up a tele-sells scenario. The selected salespeople would make calls from the office to potential clients that would purchase the company's services and products. At the interview I was asked, "Do you know anything about computers?" I said "yes" and I was hired. My start date was about two weeks away. I went to my 14-year-old son and my younger brother, both of whom were into computers, I got them to teach me how to "double-click" with a mouse and send emails, this was a very interesting and funny experience, the difficulty I had in double-clicking the mouse was pricelessly funny. It's hard to believe how long ago that was.

Anyway, in no time, I became one of the top three salespersons; and over some years things went very well. During this time, the nation experienced the dot com collapse in 2001; the company that I worked for also collapsed. Now at this time in my life, I had not fully begun to appreciate planning, preparation, time management – those very important life lessons. I was successful because I was probably making over a thousand calls a day and because I came out of a telemarketing background I didn't mind making calls, I actually enjoyed it.

So, the numbers were working for me in terms of sales that I would generate in a month's time. So much so, during the heyday of the company, I was making a substantial amount of income on the basis of closing a lot of deals. But as I said, the business collapsed under the Internet bubble that burst. Since, I had not come to any conclusion in my life by knowing how to focus on any area and making it happen, I was basically caught up in a current of life and was just rolling. Just so happens, I was doing well before things turned in the opposite direction.

I was devastated, because I always felt that on one level it wasn't my fault. It was the company and the products that were making me successful. I didn't look at it from the standpoint that it was my actions of coming in early, leaving late, making a substantial amount of calls and not quitting until I made a few more sales in a day, that would add up at the end-of-the month. This discipline allowed me to exceed my quota every time—I had gotten used to that. So in essence, some of the things I learned from my work experience are those that I apply now in my own newly-created business. It is important that you really identify with something that you are passionate about.

At 50, I had the opportunity to be in a stage play, I was asked by someone who wrote a play. When I did the performances, I got bitten by the proverbial acting bug. It had become my passion—it was something that I loved. I decided at that point, that acting was what I was going to do for the rest of my life.

Being older, I realized that for me to effectively do this, something I was passionate about, I needed to learn some things. So in my research, all of the actors that I truly respected, like Pacino, Denzel, DeNiro and other notables, all referred to stage acting as a place to really hone your skills along with training in order to become an accomplished actor. That's when I decided to invest both the time and money to learn the techniques that would make me a better actor.

I was fortunate to be in D.C. which is somewhat of a theatre town, I have been cast in over 20 plus stage productions, some of the works such as "Rossum's Universal Robots," "A Change is Gonna Come" and "8 Parts Of Life" which is the National Organ Donor Awareness production of which I am especially proud to be a cast member and co-producer. Needless to say, after seven years of performing I naturally got better as an actor. I decided I wanted to make the transition into film and television.

I then began to look around for an organization. I joined the Actors Center. They had free classes. They offered classes such as improvisation and on-camera. I knew it was time for a teacher to enhance my skills for film work. I came across a very well-known New York actor and well-publicized, on-camera acting coach, John Pallotta. He is one of the top rated acting coaches in the country. I became a member of his class—and the rest is history. I guess at 50, having had various life experiences with many types of people, I can bring realism to my acting in terms of developing characters—a technique that I learned from John and other coaches.

Recently, I decided to start a company. I wanted my company to be able to impact people's experiences by teaching them some of the techniques that we employ in acting for them to utilize in their everyday lives. This technique will work for both new and experienced actors.

There are actually four things I think are imperative to one's success. In terms of being able to impact their own circumstances, they can pretty much map out where they wish to go. I refer to it as "creating the current." The way I look at it, life is like the ocean and within the ocean there are currents that run slightly beneath the surface. If a person gets caught up in a current, much like people get caught up in life, they find themselves being taken in any direction if they don't have a clarity and a purpose as to where they wish to go.

Sometimes a person gets caught in the everyday current of going to work and coming home—day in/day out. If they don't have that thing they are passionate about, the one that drives them to make certain things happen in their lives, they will look up after 25-30 years and find they have not built anything for their family's future. To simplify, if they were to identify a current and create a current with clarity, focus and purpose—they could go from point A to point B. Much like the ancient seafarers would come from North Africa, they followed the current to bring them to North America. This is an example of utilizing existing currents.

So, what I like to do with people is to give them insight and advice to assist them in identifying their passion, and guide them to the realization of how they can basically create their own situation by the decisions they make, and how to make appropriate choices. The basic four things I believe help people to begin creating their own positive currents are:

1. Be clear on that very thing in their lives that brings them the most joy and sense of peace.
2. Identify how that which brings them the most satisfaction and return, can be shared with others that have a similar interest.
3. Be committed to learning and knowing as much about whatever they decide is their passion.
4. Associate with like-minded individuals to help gather life energy to make things happen.

These are the basic things that have allowed me to become a successful actor, producer and entrepreneur.

This is the reason that my company Black Carpet Productions was founded.

About Adiyb

Adiyb Muhammad is a native of Washington, D.C. who, after years of working successfully as a major account executive for a few technology companies, stumbled upon his passion for acting. So, at the age of 50, Adiyb began a journey that gave rise to a company Black Carpet Productions that helps aspiring playwrights get their plays produced. Adiyb has a drive to help as many actors and producers develop quality work by bringing them together to create meaningful projects with some sort of important theme. Since his initial activities, Adiyb started Black Carpet Productions and he never stopped being involved in entertainment projects. He appeared in several very popular shows on Netflix, TV One, BET and Lifetime Movie Network.

Adiyb is an avid reader of motivational and business success material and has developed a unique business coaching method for actors as they pursue their careers. "Treat it as a business with less reliance from others to reach your goals." He calls this approach simply, "Creating the current."

Adiyb has been successful in making several transitions in his life that all lead to what he calls true success doing something that helps or serves people in some way. His opportunity to co-author with Brian Tracy is a result of his "Create the Current" philosophy. This mindset changed his life forever and he began to get more joy and happiness to influence and control experiences.

Adiyb is both humbled and grateful for the opportunity to share with the world what he sees as a means to bring unimaginable contentment and fulfillment. He helps his clients by:
- providing them the insight and confidence to begin to "create the currents" in their lives.
- identifying their passion and developing a strategic approach to pursuit that passion.
- giving them tools that help them experience their success.

Adiyb speaks before groups to help them see that where they find themselves in success is an ongoing opportunity to serve and help others, for we are all connected. You can find out more about Adiyb at:
- Website: www.blackcarpetproductions
- Twitter: adiybm
- Facebook: Author Adiyb Muhammad.

CHAPTER 14

MASTERING FINANCIAL SUCCESS

BY FIJEH ROSELINE AADUM

According to a global Accenture survey conducted in July 2012, of the more than 8,000 people from 15 countries involved in the survey, only about one in six people (16 per cent) are confident that their current level of savings is sufficient to cover their financial needs after retirement. While about 93% admit that they will need to rely partly or wholly on their personal savings to cover their post-retirement financial needs, more than 67% don't know how much they would need to save to guarantee their standard of living in retirement. Furthermore, less than 29% have private investments aimed specifically at addressing their retirement needs (in addition to any employer or public pension funds from which they may benefit).[1]

Also, according to the 2015 Career Builders annual retirement survey, 54% of senior workers (age 60+) will have to work after retiring from their current career. Of this number, 81% will work part time and the other 19% will have to continue working full time.[2]

Seven in ten seniors (69%) who graduated from public and non-profit colleges in 2013 had student loan debt, with an average of $28,400 per borrower. This represents a two per cent increase from the average debt of 2012 public and non-profit graduates. Statistics also show that in 2012, 71% of all students graduating from four-year colleges had student loan debt. This figure amounts to about 1.3 million students graduating with debt up from 1.1 million in 2008 and 0.9 million in 2004.[3]

Reports also show that in 2012, 66% of graduates from public colleges had student loans, while 75% of graduates from private non-profit colleges had student loans and 88% of graduates from for-profit colleges had student loans.

These statistics are alarming!

One would expect the usual trend to be parents footing the bills of their children's education up to college level, if they can afford it. However, we find that the percentage of those whose parents cannot afford to cater for their academic demands is grossly higher.

The obvious choice being to take student loans, we see the resultant effect being a situation where thousands of students have acquired debts long before they start their first jobs. These individuals go on to spend the first two or three years of their working life repaying debts. What a way to begin!

This is on the one hand; on the other hand, let's take a look at the average work-life span of an individual. Several researchers show that the average spans over a period of 30-40 years. Usually, after that, the individual starts to make retirement plans. And if this plan is not fail-safe, there is a possibility that such a person may be forced to join the work force again.

Statistics show that up to 54% of people aged 60+ have to go back to work as stated above! This is a grim situation. This is the cruel reality we have to live with; the early part of youth or work life is spent paying debts, while the latter years, when retirement ought not to be so far away is spent 'weighing options.' One wonders when respite will ever come; when will one ever have that time to be free from active work and spend time on recreation and other productive things?

With the advent of technology and knowledge, life expectancy has improved significantly. Right from the Paleolithic age to present day, world average life expectancy has been on a steady rise. During the Paleolithic age, life expectancy was 33 years; now it is at 67.2 years. This gap can be attributed to the development of science and technology.[4]

With improved nutrition, health care and more information and awareness on healthy living, people tend to live longer now. This in turn means you need to prepare for a longer stretch of retirement years now moreso than ever before.

How do we prepare not just for retirement, but for a satisfying, productive and life-enriching retirement? How are we able to maintain financial independence through our retirement years? How do we make the years we have worked, the funds we have saved up and the commitment we have made to retire gracefully add up? How do we Master Success in our Finances?

My goal here is to help you find ways your income will outlive you, and enable you to leave something behind for the next generation.

SEVEN TIPS TO MASTER FINANCIAL SUCCESS

1. KNOW THYSELF

Confront the dark parts of yourself, and work to banish them with illumination and forgiveness. Your willingness to wrestle with your demons will cause your angels to sing.
~ August Wilson[5]

Take stock of your present situation. Do a comprehensive self-evaluation:
- What are your assets and what are your liabilities?
- What are the assets you currently have that could be a source of revenue in future?
- What are those things that are liabilities or waste in your life?

You need to also consider your income and expenditure: what are your sources of income and will that level of income sustain you later in life? Again, you need to track your expenditure earnestly. What do you spend most of your income on? Are they worthwhile? Are they adding value to your life and can that money be put to better use?

When you have carried out a proper evaluation of your current financial outlook, you are best positioned to make the changes necessary in your journey to finding financial freedom.

As Pema Chödrön pointed out in his book, *When Things Fall Apart: Heart Advice for Difficult Times,* "The most fundamental aggression to ourselves, the most fundamental harm we can do to ourselves, is to remain ignorant by not having the courage and the respect to look at ourselves honestly and gently."[6]

2. REALISE YOU NEED A PLAN

If you fail to plan, you have planned to fail.
~ Author Unknown

Planning is telling your money where to go rather than wondering where it went.
~ Oscar Wilde

No one ever sets out on a journey to a new destination without being armed with a map or a clear description of their desired destination and how to get there.[7] Having a detailed plan is a must in this journey to financial freedom. Embarking on such a journey without having a clear destination and navigation details is like the traveller who set out on a journey and when asked about his desired destination, answers in response, "I don't know exactly, but when I arrive I will know it."

The clearer and more detailed your map, the faster and smoother your journey will be. Do take out time to set out a plan of action for your financial journey and stick to it, improving wherever the need arises.

You need to start planning now for your post-retirement years. It may seem a long way off, but it is never too early to start planning.

It has been said that people will need to fund about 20 years of post-work years (i.e., between retirement at 60 and 80 years of age). That is a long time and it is important to start planning for it now.[8]

Part of planning is to consider the kind of lifestyle you wish to maintain after you stop working and how much will be needed to maintain that kind of lifestyle. Almost 30% of retirees said they did not prepare adequately for a comfortable retirement because they did not realize how much they needed to save for their retirement.

3. SET GOALS

Goal-setting is a powerful process for thinking about your ideal future, and for motivating yourself to turn your vision of this future into reality. The process of setting goals helps you choose where you want to go in life.

Setting goals helps you evaluate whether you are making progress or not. Set goals for your savings plan and how you plan to reduce expenditure. For example, you could have a goal to save $1 million in ten years; break it down into realizable targets of perhaps annual, monthly or weekly savings. That gives approximately $100,000 per annum and $8,333 per month. If you keep at it, in no time, you would have achieved your goal of a million dollars.

Be fastidious about meeting your goals because this is how you can make any meaningful progress. Remember, roadblocks to your goals don't mean failure.

4. BECOME AN INVESTOR

If you have to work for all the money you earn,
you can only go so far. Learn to give your money
the opportunity to work as hard as you work.
~ Fijeh Aadum

Investment is a key way to plan for the future; it is a good way to secure the future. It is also a good way to shore up for contingencies, unforeseen or unplanned events like accidents, sudden loss of employment, etc. The following tips will get you started – or keep you going – on your journey to becoming an investor:

a) **Have a savings culture:** This helps you to gather a good critical mass for investment. Savings helps you to build a fat substance for investment. Don't just save up money at the bank, inflation may catch up with it, have an investment plan for which you are saving.

b) **Invest in shares and stocks:** Never mind the news about the crash of the stock market that you have heard in the past; stocks and shares are still fertile areas you can put your money into. Find out and research companies whose shares are valuable and have the tendency to appreciate over time. There are companies that regardless of whatever crisis hits the stock market, their shares tend to bounce back and there are also companies whose stock value will multiply immensely and far surpass the purchasing value.

c) **Property:** Property is another area that is considered to be lucrative. Property will always appreciate in value. Find out about locations where you can buy property, i.e., locations where the possibility of future development is high. That is how to position yourself for good opportunities. Some locations may not look so attractive at the moment, but if you invest in them, by the time development and civilization catch up with them, you would be wealthy beyond your imagination.

d) **Pension scheme:** Find out about reliable and efficient pension companies or managers. Some of them have plans or packages of investing your money as they deem fit instead of just keeping it in the bank. These packages include purchasing stocks on your behalf, etc.

Remember, if you had to work for all the money you make,
you can only go so far.
~ Fijeh Aadum

Whatever you do, you must have a business by the side
that makes you money but has no employees.
~ Anthony Robbins

5. START WHERE YOU ARE WITH WHAT YOU HAVE.

The biggest personal finance mistake people make is waiting
for a pile of cash.
~ Anthony Robbins

You don't have to wait till you have all the millions before you start saving or investing or having a financial plan. Start where you are with what you have. Remember the popular saying, *little drops of water make the mighty ocean.*

This brings to mind the story of Oseola McCarty (March 7, 1908 – September 26, 1999), a local washerwoman in Hattiesburg, Mississippi who became The University of Southern Mississippi (USM)'s most famous benefactor.

McCarty drew global attention after it was announced in July 1995 that she had established a trust through which, at her death, a portion of her life's savings would be left to the university to provide scholarships for deserving students in need of financial assistance. The amount was estimated at $150,000, a surprising amount given her menial occupation.[9]

How does a local washer woman become such a huge benefactor? Her singular action generated billions of dollars from the people who were challenged by her generosity. Her secret was the fact that she knew to start small. Read more of her story in Robin Sharma's book, *Extraordinary Leadership*.

6. USE THE POWER OF COMPOUNDING

You don't earn your way to wealth; you invest your way to wealth through the power of compounding. Becoming wealthy is not an event that would suddenly happen; and even if it does, it will take knowledge and skill to manage it so that it doesn't fizzle out suddenly the way it came. Becoming wealthy is a series of actions and decisions culminating in prosperous finances.
~ Anthony Robbins.

No story better illustrates the power of compounding like that of Anne Scheiber. Anne Scheiber had a series of negative experiences with financial brokers in the 1930s, and retired from her job as an auditor at the Internal Revenue Service in the mid-1940s with only $5,000 saved up and a $3,100 pension. She then spent the next 50 years accumulating wealth by making a series of wise financial investments, share purchases, and savings.[10]

Scheiber managed to accumulate a life savings of $22 million throughout her lifetime. She was known as a frugal and eccentric woman who reportedly took food from a meeting of shareholders one time and consumed it over the next three days. Till her passing in 1995, she lived in the same apartment and wore the same clothing that she did in

1944. After she died at the age of 101, she donated her life savings to establishing scholarships for deserving girls at Yeshiva University.[11]

7. FINALLY, TALK TO AN EXPERT (GET A COACH)

You get the best effort from others not by lighting a fire beneath them, but by building a fire within.
~ Bob Nelson

Just like people have mentors or coaches for their careers and marriages, it is important to have a financial coach, someone you look to, someone who is successful financially and who can hold you accountable when it comes to finances. Carefully select a person that lights a fire inside of you, keeping your dreams alive and before you.

Finally, remember that more education is not what you need, more consultation may not be what you need, and another finance course may also not help. What you need is to START NOW, doing what you have already learnt.

Infuse your life with action. Don't wait for it to happen. Make it happen. Make your own future. Make your own hope. Make your own love. And whatever your beliefs, honour your Creator, not by passively waiting for grace to come down from upon high, but by doing what you can to make grace happen... yourself, right now, right down here on earth.
~ Bradley Whitford[12]

Do you want to know who you are? Don't ask. Act! Action will delineate and define you.
~ Thomas Jefferson[13]

Let's take Nike's advice and "JUST DO IT."

References/Endnotes

1. http://newsroom.accenture.com/news/majority-of-people-globally-are-worried-about-outliving-their-money-at-retirement-accenture-survey-finds.htm
2. Capricorn.bc.edu
3. Quick Facts About Student Debt, March 2014
4. http://en.wikipedia.org/wiki/Life_expectancy
5. http://www.goodreads.com/quotes/tag/self-assessment
6. http://www.goodreads.com/quotes/tag/self-assessment
7. http://www.goodreads.com/quotes/tag/self-assessment
8. The Future of Retirement Global Report A balancing act, by HSBC
9. https://en.wikipedia.org/wiki/Oseola_McCarty
10. Anne Scheiber http://en.wikipedia.org/wiki/Anne_Scheiber
11. http://beginnersinvest.about.com/od/ investorsmoneymanagers/a/Anne_Scheiber.htm
12. http://www.brainyquote.com/quotes/keywords/action.html
13. http://www.brainyquote.com/quotes/keywords/action.html

About Fijeh Roseline

Fijeh Roseline Aadum is a seasoned Financial Adviser and an entrepreneur taking on multiple roles as a Business Consultant, Speaker, Writer and Life Coach.

Fijeh has taught and trained business owners, aspiring entrepreneurs and employees, on Business start-up and success, Human Potential Development, Personal Development, Personal Finance, and other topical issues locally and Internationally.

A strong believer in the limitless potential of Man, Fijeh founded 'The Value Centre' with a vision to *empower* people to self-realization, *inspire and empower* people to bring out the very best in them and give them the opportunity and platform to give back or impact their world.

Fijeh Roseline is the Country Representative for Abana Group International, a respected Financial Advisory Institution that specializes in helping Individuals, families and Institutions attain their Financial and Business Expansion Goals.

Fijeh Roseline Aadum holds an MBA in International Business from one of UK's premier Business Schools and is a member of several professional bodies, including The CFIP and CII among others. She is a John Maxwell Certified Coach and Speaker.

She is guest contributor in the online magazine 'virtue digest.'

She is married to Godswill Aadum and they have 3 children.

CHAPTER 15

THE ENTREPRENEURIAL CONSULTANT

BY ANDREAS BUENTER

[For entrepreneurial consultants seeking more recognition, more serenity, and more money – be it as a start-up, in an established company, or to surpass the milestone of 1 million in revenue.]

Do the right thing, the right way, and actually do it.

This slogan was passed on to me by Sam Brunner. Sam is an exceptionally gifted management consultant with a wide range of clients. Passionate. Analytical. Tough. And fully booked. I first met him in 1992 during my first serious crisis as a consulting start-up. One year earlier, when I was 28 years old, I quit my very well-paid position as a senior financial analyst at a renowned Swiss private bank and started my own company as a financial consultant. It was time to bring an independent voice for evaluating private equity and stock investments to the market.

I started out in the consulting business for investors charging per daily or hourly rate. Later on, we decided to grow the business with periodicals, i.e., monthly print publications in the pre-digital world. Together with Norman Rentrop's publishing team, my team and I worked hard seven days a week to establish the first independent research service for institutional and private investors, a printed informational product, periodical, covering over 430 international publically-traded companies on a monthly basis. Despite the effort, I was running out of cash. I was in the middle of hundreds of pages of research manuscripts, building a gigantic database of company data, and employing a dozen people.

The only thing that I instinctively realized at the time, "If it doesn't work, I just have to increase my input, cash, and time." Being an entrepreneur requires a dream and stamina, at least that's what everyone says. Sure, but Samuel taught me to focus on something else. When you're under stress, breathe deeply through your nose four times and reflect on these questions for ten minutes:

- Am I doing the right thing?
- Am I doing it in the right way?
- Am I actually doing it?

I had to increase prices dramatically. The value-price-relationship was out of order. The deal with the publisher was re-negotiated.

This led not just to a doubling in revenue to a higher six-figure amount within the year, it also prepared my company for a merger, which turned me into a temporary millionaire.

But there is more I want to teach you, than just increasing prices. I believe that every self-employed management consultant / entrepreneur has the right to discover a reliable, repeatable system that brings the recognition, the safety, and the money that he or she deserves.

So, let's have a look at the success-critical themes: Over the course of your career, you have collected great amounts of know-how, expertise, and experience. However, when you approach your potential customers, you are competing against dozens of consultants with regard to your positioning. To better differentiate yourself, an approach may be that "my services / solutions have to differentiate especially through 'technical competence' and 'ability'. I will present these strengths at every introductory meeting, bolstered with PowerPoint slides and more." This was my approach for a while.

And it was a big mistake!

And then there are the *price / fee negotiations*. "My potential clients calculate their target price for my services like this: How many hours / days will he / she need, multiplied by a certain hourly rate that one has heard from friends in c-level positions, equals expected execution costs, plus profit margin, equals price. Everyone does it like this, so I am doing it correctly." You may consider: This limit to your profit is as high and thick as a dam wall in the Swiss Alps. Insurmountable.

Let me briefly comment on the topic of *Marketing and Sales*. Regardless of whether you are the sole proprietor or if you are building a company with a revenue of more than 1 million annually with the goal of later selling it (this was my aim). As a start-up, we wanted to grow to reach a crucial size. As an established entrepreneur and founder, I had to at least replace the completed projects. At the time, I hated sales. I only "did" sales & marketing when the last projects were settled since it was high time for a fresh supply of projects. Since everyone else was doing the same, I was convinced that I was doing it right. A big mistake that limited my company to triviality.

Another topic that often sparks controversial discussions in forums: When I began being self-employed, I decided to work alone, without the burden of managing people and paying monthly salaries and other fix costs. However, I still needed additional know-how or simply resources to optimally fulfill the customers' requirements. My "leadership principles" at the time were as follows: 1) "People who work with me, be it as freelancers or as employees, should know themselves what they should be doing when. It cannot be my daily routine to follow-up. 2) If it's of high priority, I will rather take the task myself and deal with the client directly." Does this sound familiar?

Even as a graduate financial analyst, CIIA, and with a degree in business administration, I had – in retrospect – a funny approach regarding **finances** as an entrepreneur. "Planning, measuring, optimizing using calculations with regard to marketing, sales, and liquidity planning, are tools for big companies. I don't have time for this bureaucracy, so I will do it later when the company has grown." Now, the relationship between the marketing plan, sales channel, and liquidity plan helps me stay relaxed during stressful times. Who is to do it?

The two Excel sheets that support your planning are updated every Monday morning before the team meeting. In this meeting, you may discuss the client projects with your staff. In case there are some delays, these are immediately considered in the liquidity plan. The updated marketing and sales plan is incorporated in the columns for expected revenue. This way, you have an overview of probable incoming payments from existing clients and the values from newly-acquired customers that are exposed to risk. Possible changes with regard to costs are also considered.

I would like to once again ask you "what is the right thing, what is the right way to do it, and what is actually important" with regard to positioning and sales. You have probably heard that people's purchasing decision is based "90% on emotional reasons" rather than objective reasons.

As a consultant with in-depth expert knowledge, you will quickly fall into a sales trap when you tell your potential client the following at the first meeting: "We are reliable, experienced, have a long history, and work for these clients." Then you look out for "purchasing signals in his or her gestures and few words." However, presenting such a "sales pitch" is not at all interesting at this point in time! My sales coach from Chicago, Gene Rosendale, founder of nonselling.com, brutally demonstrated this. Every statement of this kind leads your counterpart responding with a natural defense mechanism. "I have to think about it" is the mildest form of your sales effort that just fizzles out. No response, and decisions are delayed. This is a common sales efficiency killer, isn't it?

Prospective customers hate salesmen, because they always assume that their offer is so good that it must fit the customer. They talk too much. They ask investigative questions. They do not seem interested in the person's environment and situation, their views, perspectives, emotions, and priorities. If you could stop selling like this, your sales efficiency would increase by 100 to 300% with the same effort. That means more recognition, less frustration, and more money for the same effort.

Here is a trick that could help you not to sell. You could start every initial meeting with an assumption, your view to find out more about your counterpart, his or her surroundings and work. It's about him or her.

150

No small talk. No elevator pitch. No selling. No branding.

People love responding to your assumptions and correcting your point of view. For example, "…nice to meet you. I saw on your LinkedIn profile that… the company is respected by the market as a reliable supplier… you have done a lot to establish yourself…" PAUSE. It is almost guaranteed that your counterpart will pick up the conversation and start a dialogue.

In the following minutes, you will actively steer the dialogue. Your remarks and questions always refer to what your counterpart previously said. It's all about him or her, not you. For example, "Interesting. What do you mean by that?" or "Could you explain that to me again?" or "You haven't mentioned XYZ, what does that mean?" This way, you can gather relevant information (about time, money, problems, market) as long as you like without giving your counterpart the impression of being interviewed by purpose.

Then you move on. You can summarize what was said at any time, and then insert a 15-second advertisement. For example, "With all these issues, you have a really exciting position. You have achieved this and that… maybe I can contribute towards achieving this and that…" PAUSE and wait for an answer.

The prospective customer will then probably ask you, "What is the price" or "What are next steps?" He or she is in the lead. In dialogue, not through sales talk. By the way, you should never bring a PowerPoint presentation to the first meeting since you cannot know the customer's detailed needs in advance.

This dialogue model allows you to strongly distinguish yourself from the competition! The effects on your business can be manifold: Trust is built up more quickly. You have control over the conversation at any time without being controlling. You don't feel like a salesman. You receive information that you previously didn't have. Prospective customers regularly tell you that "we had an interesting conversation." Voila!

Now on to pricing. My position is that prospective customers only wants to see a price in relation to his or her benefit in order to satisfy his or her reasoning. Emotionally, the prospect has already decided on you since you didn't sell.

What is the meaning of benefit-based pricing? If you can change your client's strategy in a way that increases his or her profit by USD 253,187 annually in just one hour – based on your experience and knowledge – would you charge just one hour?

There are two alternatives to this scenario. You could charge a 'flat rate' for the completion of the assignment based on the expected results. Your risk: the effort can explode beyond the planned scope. To get an o.k. to a 'flat rate' you should consider the calculated expected financial effect (the result) is shown first, the remuneration last. Another option is to 'share the future result' (often called "success fee"), but to charge a fee in case the project is cancelled (a "cancellation fee"). If you are brave, you can offer a guarantee: "no remuneration without success."

All business people will tell you that getting more customers, increased prices, and higher purchasing frequency are the only three ways to increase revenue. However, you should also consider the closing rate in your sales process. How many meetings can you schedule out of 10 important contacts (by phone, e-mail)? 1 out of 10 = 10% or 2 out of 10 = 20%? This constitutes a difference of 100% while exerting the same effort. How many meetings lead to how many deals? Improving this performance indicator, the conversion ratio, has a huge impact since more revenue can be generated from the same input.

I simply measure this and other performance indicators on a piece of paper in my paper notebook. No software necessary!

Finally, let me return to the topic of leadership. "People who work with me have to know what they should be doing." Don't leave the future up to chance! This will cost you a fortune in terms of health (negative stress), recognition (customer satisfaction), and money (cash and hours spent). Every freelancer and employee needs a clear job description, clear-cut and unambiguous assignments at the beginning of the week and controlling at the end of the week. This is a simple planning and leadership process that you should apply to your own work. Every Friday, you may recapitulate for 15 minutes to note down what went well, what has to improve, and you communicate these notes at the beginning of the following week! If people regularly deviate from targets set? Make a change. The weekly review is a scheduled meeting in Outlook or any other calendar you may prefer.

Before you start a new week, you should think about and consider the following seven action steps:

1. 20% talking, 80% listening = trusted advisor.
2. Sales without selling increases results by factors, shown by the sales elite.
3. Use the system of benefit-based-pricing to increase your profitability.
4. Tie liquidity planning together with marketing and sales planning.
5. Leadership = communicating clear, measurable, and achievable goals.
6. Leadership = Evaluating achievements in review, optimizing and drawing consequences.
7. Increase your conversion rate rather than scheduling more meetings.

About Andreas

Andreas Buenter helps his clients to transform their business to get to a new level in cost and sales efficiency. Growing up in Switzerland, he was always interested in numbers, and how businesses work. That's why he began his career with a commercial internship with a regional bank in Lucerne. He then developed a passion for investment research in various positions in international private banking. In 1991, Andreas founded his first consulting company with regard to the topic of independent investment research, sector and company analyses. Within eight years, he worked on more than 3,000 company analyses from over 20 industries. Running analyses, creative development of options, clear recommendations, improving existing workflows, and inspiring people continue to be his passions today.

With the increasing success of his own business, and temporarily large setbacks, the demands on marketing, sales, leadership, people and financial management, restructuring, M&A (mergers and acquisitions) steadily increased. Today, Andreas' consulting business encompasses international clients of all sizes, from individual management consultants to owners of family businesses and CFOs of publically-listed corporations.

Andreas Buenter is fluent in German, English, French, and Swiss-German. He is a qualified bank officer, he studied further after business hours to become a business economist, and he is a certified financial analyst and asset manager as well as CIIA (Certified International Investment Analyst). He is the founder and partner of Buenter Management Ltd., a consulting and private equity boutique based near Zurich, Switzerland. The company is also a partner, and Andreas is the Area Director Switzerland, of Expense Reduction Analysts, an organization that – together with 700 partners worldwide – is a leading consulting company for reducing indirect costs. In 2016, Andreas was also the founder of www.GetYourExpert.com, a knowledge, referral, and advanced business training platform for consultants from both management and other disciplines.

Furthermore, he is the partner of the M&A consulting company MilleniumAssociates Ltd. based in Zurich and London. For over 10 years, he was Chief Analyst of the market-leading publication *Die Aktien-Analyse* (The Stock Analyst), which has several thousand readers and is published by the Verlag für die Deutsche Wirtschaft AG based in Bonn, Germany.

Andreas has held talks and keynotes about sales, corporate finance and entrepreneurship in Switzerland, Germany, Italy, Spain, Great Britain, and Qatar. He is a regular contributor to blogs. He is an accredited sales coach and developed the

"9 Step Sales Process" for consultants of Expense Reduction Analysts in Europe. He is the winner of the 2013 Silver, and 2014 as well as 2015 Gold Award for Outstanding Achievements in Sales and Client Management, and the 2014 Winner of the Quality Award by his peers.

Depending on your area of interest, you can contact Andreas at:
- ab@buenter.ch
- abuenter@expensereduction.com
- andreas.buenter@getyourexpert.com
- www.twitter.com/andreasbuenter
- www.facebook.com/andreasbuenter

CHAPTER 16

BRINGING CLARITY TO OUR LIVES

– I FINALLY GOT IT RIGHT

BY AMANDA WOODWARD

We all have a purpose, and mine is to help others create personal and physical environments that help them be at their best.

My life wasn't always clear cut and easily defined. I was surrounded by all those "convenient choices" we all have for easier living. Fast foods, quick solutions, and the promise of convenience. But convenience does come at a price—often our health. This is a message that is often preached, but seldom absorbed. And no country refuses to accept the downside of convenience quite so much as the United States.

Through the good grace of God, I have been blessed with insight that helps me to see the world we live in differently than many do. *I'm able to go back to "in the beginning" and look at how things have changed from a different perspective than many have.* **To be specific, health problems and being spiritually grounded are struggles for many people.** They have lost their instinctual ability to balance their physical and emotional worlds, creating chaos at every turn.

We live in a country that should be amazing by everyone's standards. People long to come here and every year they find a way. Why is that? At the heart of it I see one major reason: *We are America, one nation under God.* But somehow God has been left out of the biggest decisions in many of our lives, making us less aware of the consequences. It's no wonder why so many people are suffering and longing for solutions that never come.

God has already created in nature everything that we need to live happy, healthy, and abundant lives. It's up to us to find it.

Inspired by love for my fellow man and an obligation to use my God-given gifts, my goal is one that comes from the heart. I want to help connect people to the messages that will help them recognize how important it is for them to return to more organic living and mindfulness of the choices they make. This presents a big question: *Why choose what is processed when we have natural choices that have been around on this earth since its creation?*

OUR PHYSICAL ENVIRONMENTS DO IMPACT OUR EMOTIONAL WELLBEING

We are only human, which means we inwardly carry what happens to us outwardly.

When things happen to us—even things beyond our control—our human tendency is to hold on to those things, trying to process them and solve the difficulties all on our own. Our free will runs strong and we cling to it with everything we have, often struggling against the spiritual approach to healing and health.

When it comes to our physical environments, they do have a great impact on our emotional wellbeing. Far too often people use products and eat food that our bodies retaliate against. We get health problems. *Think about this...*

- We use cleaning products that are made from chemicals, despite there being ingredients out there that are natural, which means they are better for our health.

- We often eat or drink products that have ingredients we cannot even pronounce in them. For example, some beverages contain an ingredient called Brominated Vegetable Oil. This ingredient makes dyes and flavors stick to water. It's also an ingredient that is banned in over 100 countries (but not the US).

- Chronic diseases such as Asthma and Diabetes have been linked to the products we consume and use in our physical environments. Studies and years of research also show links to cancer and ADD.

Every one of those scenarios above are an outcome that has to do with using manmade products, versus the healthier alternative—God-made products. And these harmful ingredients are in more products than what we maybe even realize, including: body and skin care products, cosmetics, laundry soap, perfumes, toothpaste and mouthwash, dish washing detergent, and even carpet cleaners (those same carpets you like to keep "clean" for your little treasures).

Furthermore, when we get sick, it cannot help but consume our thoughts, which brings down our emotional wellbeing. The symptoms can be impossible to avoid. Fatigue. Severe weight loss or weight gain. Cramps, aches, and pains. And many more!

CHOOSING LONGEVITY OVER CONVENIENCE
Our best efforts often fail when they are rooted in false beliefs.

I am someone who has always strived to do my best at everything I chose to do, and I thought I was doing a pretty good job. With a natural love for networking with people and seeking out business opportunities around things I enjoyed, I was a representative for a jewelry business that helped people tell their life stories through their creations, a stamping and scrapbooking business, as well as other businesses that helped other people find joy while allowing me to make a great living. *After all, we love our careers more when we see how we are helping our family.* **This is why I was shocked when I began to learn about how convenience was impacting the people I loved most—those who inspired me to work hard every day.**

I'll never forget that day. It was not that long ago—June 2nd, 2015—and these two sweet women came to my home to talk about their business. *They looked sweet and were delightful, but what they shared with me terrified me!* They talked about how most of us just purchase cleaning products at a local store. For "convenience," of course. What most consumers didn't realize was that the products they purchased often shared a direct link to chronic ailments and concerns. **I didn't want to "just believe them." After all, if I did, I'd have to admit where I'd really faltered in truly protecting and doing the best I could do for my children and husband.** After my own research, I found this information :

> Many harsh acidic (low pH) or basic (high pH) cleaners aggravate asthma symptoms because they irritate the lungs. Moreover, if improperly mixed, bleach and acidic or ammonia-based cleaners can react to form extremely high concentrations of chlorine gas, which can cause a person to develop asthma after a single intense exposure (AOEC 2012). Other chemicals, like quats (quaternary ammonium compounds), bleach and ammonia, can cause asthma through allergic reactions that develop slowly after frequent, long-term exposures to lower concentrations of the substances. (Bernstein 2006 ; AOEC 2012).

Ouch! What a wake-up call and this just scratches the surface. I hope you get the idea of what I'm talking about. Assuredly, I don't build my career around scaring people, but rather by informing them of how they can make smarter choices that serve their families, their environments, and show God that they've taken notice of the solutions He's had for us all along.

By helping to educate people on how convenience is not aligned with longevity, I love helping guide people to better solutions that improve their lives—inside and out. It's the inspiration behind I Finally Got It Right, INC. And guess what? Now that I've gotten it right, it's incredible how much easier it has become to help others get it right, too.

It's not about judgment; it's about a genuine desire to help my fellow man have a better quality of life. It is about awareness.

BRINGING AWARENESS AND PROMOTING WELLNESS

I used to sell things that I believed in, but my days of selling are over. Today I am able to show and demonstrate to people how their lives will be better. It speaks for itself!

When you believe in something and are excited about it there is no struggle to practice what you speak. By veering away from convenience and placing my focus on the natural as compared to the synthetic, I saw results right away for my family. It was a powerful testimonial to how some basic information can quite literally be revolutionary in nature. And I wasn't the only one to notice—my entire family sensed the benefits, too. Not even factoring in lifestyle choices aside from how I cleaned my home, this is what happened:

- There were fewer illnesses in our house over this past year, including colds, stuffiness, flu, and upset stomachs.

- The house smelled fantastic, and it wasn't due to some chemical-laden spray or product—it was natural and fresh just like nature intended.

- I had no dry hands and skin from working with chemical products to create that clean environment that was important to me.

- The concern for having my small children accidentally get into the cleaning products was eliminated—they're still in a safe place, but it gives a peace of mind that you cannot place a value on.

Regardless of how much you have chosen convenience over nature in the past, those four points are ones that resonate with us all. I am yet to meet someone that is excited about sickness, dry hands, and the thought of their kids getting a hold of something they shouldn't.

Having evidence that this "stuff" really did work and delivered what it promised, I knew there was one choice left for me—to bring this into my business platform. It was the easiest decision I've ever made, and my passion for it, backed up by the chance to "see for yourself" has given endless testimonials to how great natural cleaning products are. You really can't tell the difference until you try it. And as they say, "Try it. You'll like it." **Only in this case—you'll love it and be showing some serious love to your family at the same time.**

There were six major tenets that I wanted to be a part of my business platform, in addition to offering household cleaning products, health and beauty aids, laundry products, and an ever-increasing line of options that are natural and better for you. Each and every one of my products and what I want to offer people is important to me, because I want everyone to know how much I truly care about their health and have their best interests at heart. I couldn't imagine doing it any other way. Here they are:

1. Show that natural products can work better than the leading chemical products that are sold today.

2. Debunk the myth that it costs more to clean with natural products than the leading store- bought products most people gravitate toward.

3. Products that are 100% naturally created are good for you.

4. Offering a money back guarantee. I'm not here to "sell." I'm here to help people draw their own conclusions of how natural solutions are worth it, compared to the convenience of running down to the store to buy whatever chemical cleaner is on sale.

5. Deliver better convenience by having ways to order products online or by telephone—any time of day or night.

6. Have an efficient delivery system where people can receive their natural products within three to four days maximum—from our warehousing location to your home.

When you really are committed to helping people it is so easy to go out of your way to offer products and services that will help them—and make it an easy process. *Nobody wants difficult and challenging, but everyone does want great products at a reasonable price that are there when they need them.* These tenets have led to me meeting some truly incredible people. And without me recognizing the link between God and my gifts and how I can serve my fellow man, none of it would have been possible.

WE CAN ALL GET IT RIGHT
Let our conscious lead us to where our best choices exist.

The name of my business—I Finally Got It Right, INC.—is the only name that made sense for me. *I've loved doing the research and legwork to find the products that will help others.* I love to tell them about everything I do and the passion behind it, of course, but when something speaks for itself, it becomes that much more powerful. The products and services I offer to others does speak for itself.

I've referenced this before, but it does bear repeating because it is that important! **Each and every answer that we need to live happy and healthy lives in this world was created in the beginning, by God himself.** He didn't put these amazing gifts in this world to not be used. *Everything does serve a purpose. It's up to all of us to make sure the purpose is good.*

About Amanda

Amanda Bevill-Woodward helps her clients and customers to live happier and healthier lives daily. Being brought up around a family in sales, but a product of Generation Y, Amanda naturally gravitated to this new world of online sales.

Amanda began her sales profession by being an independent scrapbooking and card-making demonstrator with a company who creates, teaches, and sells some of the world's best supplies and tools. Amanda also helped people 'tell their stories through jewelry,' worked as an independent consultant with an online energy provider, sold an all-natural cosmetic line, but now is simply working to help others live the happiest and healthiest lives they possibly can – with an Online Wellness Company that has never seen a down-month in over 30 years, and is consistently helping serve over a million happy and satisfied customers monthly.

Amanda is a graduate of Hannibal LaGrange College in Hannibal, MO. She is the CEO of I Finally Got It Right, INC.™ Amanda is also a multi-best-selling author including *Masters of Success,* which she co-authored with Brian Tracy. She was also selected as one of America's PremierExperts™ and has been quoted in *Newsweek, The Wall Street Journal, USA Today,* and *Inc. Magazine* as well as featured on NBC, ABC, and CBS television affiliates speaking on social media, search engine optimization and making more money online.

Amanda, an ordinary person, just like so many of you, has worked with some of America's greatest professionals in the world, such as Brian Tracy, Shelli Gardner, Chrissy & Bella Weems, John Maxwell, Jere Thompson Jr., Chris Chambless, and others.

You can connect with Amanda at:
- IFinallyGotItRight@gmail.com
- www.IFinallyGotItRight.com
- www.facebook.com/IFinallyGotItRight1

CHAPTER 17

PRINCIPLES OF LIFE
– LEAVE A SUCCESSFUL LEGACY

BY ROLANDO N. MARTINEZ VELEZ

"Time" has been called the "Essence of Life." As I matured, I learned to value time. My waste of productive and precious time in my youth is a matter I wish that others could avoid. Let me give you the background and you will see what I mean. I come from a middle-class family from the southern part of Puerto Rico. As you may be aware, Puerto Rico is currently going through severe financial hardship. Seeing people leave the island in massive numbers due to the high unemployment rate is very disheartening. My hope is that my story will inspire passion, success and love for others.

In my early years there was nothing to worry about, just to get to class and pass a test of whatever curriculum subject they offered. I didn't even care what grade I had in middle school, then in high school, teachers efforts to reinforce the class were remarkable, but I was not wise enough to take advantage of my age at that time. I have to admit that even today I'm regretting all the wasted years that I have allowed to pass for no reason. But intention is not everything – teachers never told me how to plan for the future, and how life changes. There's no security in any job. I have learned that reality through hardship, and from making mistakes that have taken away the most valuable asset we have: "Time."

Oh my gosh, at this time I still feel guilty for letting that happen. I lost 10 or 12 years of my life living without purpose, asking myself, "Why do we have to suffer?" I really didn't understand anything around me. I was just breathing, eating because I felt hungry and sleeping because of my physiological needs. At one time I didn't believe in anything. . . I mean anything. I was lost, I didn't care about anything. Obviously, someone who felt that way will start becoming depressed or worse. No matter what field you're in, you have to imagine or use your imagination to create different methods in order to get people to know your story. That's what life is all about, to have something to reach out with. Nothing is impossible. On the other hand, if you don't have anybody to mentor you on how to grow in times of crisis, it is very hard to find your own way. That's one of the main reasons we get into so much trouble in life, which is why we develop emotional distress. If you don't have a passion or something to believe in, you're in trouble – a ship without an anchor; so find it, go ahead and visualize yourself being happy doing what you like. Give love to others and you will receive it back.

That's what I experienced since my life turned in a way I didn't expect, when I realized that my passion was to become a nurse and help others. After I reached 29 years of age, I suddenly had a feeling of unimaginable satisfaction that took possession of my soul. Since that time, I have lived in a favorable way of thankfulness and given thanks to God. Doing things differently help me achieve better goals in life – realizing the unique molecular structures that we are, complex systems of organs that work together for the same goal. That happened when I started taking classes in human anatomy and physiology that I took personally. Every time we took a test, I visualized my own body as the one that I was studying or exploring. In lab class, just seeing a real heart and looking at the way the mitral valve looks inside of us, and learning every day that we are alive just because of God. I also believe in the power of attraction and how it works in mysterious ways just to let you know that there's a passion inside of you, something that every human being is connected to, so if every one of us on this planet worked together, we could change the path of the earth dramatically.

I took advantage of that connection, and day-by-day, thinking of ways to improve my wellbeing, knowing that if I'm connected to God or that Great Source, he will lead me to greatness – and that's 100% guaranteed. But in order to start on your path to success, you have to believe and know that there is a power stronger than you have—one that we don't see, but only feel; one that controls everything in this universe, including every cell structure within us. That power is in every one of us and you can use it to develop yourself, change the planet, or for evil things (like addictions) if you are not in tune with that super-force called GOD. You need to know that, no matter what you think, whether there's a God or not, it doesn't matter, just because you think it is not there, it doesn't disappear. The Source is still floating in every atom or particle, even in your brain, so I invite you to take advantage of this information.

This doesn't have anything to do with any specific religion. God doesn't have a religion, God is love, so every time you do something that is positive that helps another human being, the "Source" called God that is inside every one of us, attracts positive vibrations, so you have to do it from your heart, not waiting for a response or a gift. If you do it naturally, it will happen naturally.

So when I became aware of the real Presence that represents God in our own body, or in society, I really changed the way I was thinking. Even when taking a shower, you need to be careful of what you are thinking, and what is your innermost communication, because you are talking to God or in His Presence. So, as a nurse, when I'm taking care of a patient, I see it like I am taking care of myself, or my parents. That's the purpose that we are created for—we have to take care of each other. Do you really think that every human is different? I don't think so. All of us came from that Great Source. We are part of something bigger than we are. So if you are reading this and you work in the medical field, every time that you deal with an unstable patient, please be aware of what I am saying. Be aware that everything you do for others you are doing for yourself. It is going to return to you, in a positive or negative way. It all depends on how your mind is tuned. If you just walk, talk, hear or do anything aimlessly, and you are not aware of how you really are doing things, you are going to fail just by not understanding that you are **NOT** on your own.

So if you want to succeed in life, please be aware that you are NOT alone. Be careful of your thinking, be careful what you say, because God is everywhere. Be creative, because when you create, it's not you; it's from a power bigger than you are, as you are given the tools to do anything. I have implemented this principle in my life, and it simply drastically changed everything (not my past, of course), but my future is in a spiral of well-being, I just feel happy for the simple things in life. When I see a patient breathing well, or when I ask a patient if the pain is gone, they do not always say yes, but when they do, and I was responsible for taking the pain away, it's a feeling of a high, one that no drug or stimulant can give you. That feeling that am talking about is released because you are connected to a spirit, a Commander who creates everything and wants good, and everything that you do for others He recognizes as an act of love. So you are responsible for staying in tune with our Creator and you have to be in harmony with your Source in order to succeed in life. I am telling you, it's the simple things in life that make you rich, you are not here to be unhappy or to be miserable.

So what I've learned from life I cannot expresses even with words, but I can try to tell you some of my principles and give you some advice in order to get in touch with your soul. First thing I do when I wake up is to say, "Thank you, God" just for letting me think and breathe. This simple inner talking, every single day, as simple as you think it is, is the first step to tell your body that it is alive and awake. Remember that body and soul are different, but you need to be in harmony with both of them; you cannot plan a life of success if you don't recognize that everything you are is not only what you see, but also what you feel.

Every one of us has a purpose in life, I discovered mine not long ago. I wish I could go back and replace those years I wasted, or the things I did without a real purpose, with these good intentions.

Not only do I know they are good intentions, but knowing where they are coming from, that's why I am pushing forward and advising: "Do SOMETHING, but do it with PASSION, and most importantly, GIVE CREDIT TO THE CREATOR. He doesn't have a name, believe me, this Power that creates every atom, cares more about us, and how we treat each other, and not by the name you selected to call him."

My mission is to provide care for you, not to know if you can pay me or not. I want to redesign how health care is provided. I know that Obamacare has taken some steps forward, but there are some people that are not in tune with themselves, so they can't help to achieve this universal right of being in good health – that's the way of thinking we all have to share, it's in our hands. There are some types of success in life, but there is an order in which to go: first, take care of yourself;

second, know that your body is a piece of engineering so perfect that it is not replaceable. For example, what about your lungs? If you smoke you know that you are wrong, and you are hurting yourself! Did you know how many cells work together in order to exchange oxygen? Millions. Just to let you know, I'm just saying that if you don't take care of your own body, how are you going to take care of business? That's the first milestone to understand – yourself.

Think about what it would take to create a human body? And, another thing is, your surroundings, your fellow man, it doesn't matter if it is your family, a boyfriend or a girlfriend, treat them like you would like them to treat you. It is like going back to basics because that's how you are going to make it. As soon you start doing simple things in the right way, you are going to live the right way in every single aspect of your life—business, family, socially and economically. Your mind runs your life, so think positively, and wish everyone goodness, wellness and health. It will come back to you like a boomerang, because the Power that I am talking about is something that is fair, always fair, and it is in within ourselves. So watch it, I've seen it happen to myself many times, and now that I just started to recognize that there is a God everywhere we are, I just can't stop walking in the right direction of fairness.

That's why I am so energized about the idea that healthcare needs to change. Everyone in the field of medicine needs to give back, I know it's hard having school loans to pay and having a family, but as long as life is in our hands we need to provide care, and do it with passion. So start thinking about what you are going to do, but start it now! Success in every aspect needs to be emphasized, this is a word so huge that this book, even along with all my other colleagues, cannot explain it all. *The only one thing we need to agree on is that we are here and we need to leave a legacy, a contribution to humanity of real magnitude.* So assume responsibility, put your boots on and start the journey now, be the commander of your destiny like you're supposed to. Always think of what you can do well without feeling sloppy.

Remember that if you're happy, I am happy too, so embrace this idea and you will become one of our leaders of the future. Don't forget to stay connected with your spirit, that's the real you, don't lose focus. Start an exercise routine. You don't need to start running, but at least keep moving; try to stay active and then you can increase your routine little by little, and then start doing morning jogs that will help increase your blood flow to the brain, and new ideas will come up. Concentrate when you have a goal and start to look up ways to finish your goal in a consistent manner. Manage yourself realizing that every gesture counts – how you sit, how you walk and how you say things – and people are going to notice.

That's the only way we will surpass this age of selfishness. Even though we have achieved great technologies we need to improve our own minds, and get our brains updated – that's how we are going to really evolve as a society, and change our position in civilization. We need to open our minds and think about being part of something bigger, the universe. I don't represent any organization or religion. These are my own words and represent the kind of society I want for the generations to come. We all have what it takes to be happy, that's what really matters when talking about success; if you are healthy, I am healthy.

I have to admit that life is not easy or simple, it has never been. So don't get me wrong, I am not trying to say that life is easy, I know that better than anyone. Now that you have decided to take a step forward, you are going to encounter frustrating situations, and some people will try to make you fail. Don't get mad, stay calm, positive and always know who you are. I am trying to get my message across that if you do things the right way – from your heart and not because someone told you – you are going to get more done faster than you can ever imagine.

It's not about the money you make, it's about feeling at peace in your heart, loving people and helping them. That's the only way you can achieve things, complete projects and everything else you want to. When you get to that point, you will notice that money is not important, but peace of mind is everything, The Creator made us like that, period. Look, I know it is going to be hard to change your behaviors. I know it, I've been there and I would never go back, disappointing friends, family and everyone else. Stay with these basic **Principles of Life.**

About Rolando

Rolando N. Martinez Velez is a registered nurse from Ponce, Puerto Rico. He was born and raised in Ponce to a family of strong Catholic-based parents. Felix R. Martinez Rolon, his father, worked as a Project Manager, and his mother, Carmen L. Velez Ramos, who worked as secretary of the court. He came from a middle-class family who provided no luxuries in life, but taught him the fear of God. With his brother Felix R. Martinez Velez, he went to Santa Teresita Elementary and Middle school. After graduating from San Conrado High School in Ponce, he attended Pontifical Catholic University of Puerto Rico and he started a Bachelor's degree in Public Administration. He was a fair student who didn't have any idea what his real passion was. He then moved and started working at the Magic Kingdom in Orlando, Florida as a College Program offered – where he worked as a park greeter. After six months, he then returned to his Alma Matter so that he could finished his Bachelor's degree. He then took a job in a hotel and casino where he lost focus and started working 40 hr. work weeks. He stayed working as a bartender and waiter, and stopped attending classes while making a regular basic salary that only was enough to survive. That's when he decided to enter cinematography and music school in Bayamon, Puerto Rico where he studied to be a sound engineer.

He then made a decision to go into basic training for the army while still in college, where he earned the Achievement Medal. When he returned from basic training, he was part of the 1243rd Transportation Company when the National Guard offered him tuition assistance – giving Rolando the opportunity to finish his prior Bachelor degree in Public Administration. He attributed his mindset vision of self-development and discipline to the basics he learned in the Army, and from the strong basic Christian principles that his parents taught him. His faith in God and his determination made him find his real purpose in life. He achieved his goal of becoming a Registered Nurse while reinventing both his clinical and intellectual capacities.

In 2012, he graduated from the Pontifical Catholic University of Puerto Rico where he obtained a Bachelor's degree in Public Administration. Right after he finished his first Bachelor's degree, he discovered his deep vocation as a nurse; he then started his second Bachelor's degree in Nursing Science where he attended for the next three years, graduating and making his vision a reality. Now Rolando has become a motivational speaker, an author of a bestselling book and an entrepreneur.

CHAPTER 18

THE UNTOLD POWER OF THE 3-TIERED COMPREHENSIVE SALES APPROACH

BY ROE HUBBARD

In this exclusive chapter of Masters of Success, I will share with you a unique three-tiered comprehensive sales approach that allowed my simple startup company to bring in over $15 million dollars in revenue in my first five years; it got me on as a host of "Car Lot Rescue" on Spike TV, A&E and it helped me become an owner/ CEO of the #1-endorsed Automotive Sales Event company in America, Members Only Automotive.

From "pitchin' in the kitchen" to now owning a large marketing and training firm in downtown Chicago, I will give you the fundamental building blocks and framework for building a sales event, a movement with a cause, or a business revolution that taps into the masses of people to rally behind your local event, or sales initiatives to help you meet your goals and live the life you've always dreamed of.

It's very rare that people are living the life they desire or meeting their financial goals. We all know it's the fear of criticism from others, or their fear and anxiety of failure, or lack of work ethic that stops people's ambitions – but everyone owns their own reality. . . they own their own truth. Last I checked, you can't deposit excuses! To get to the top you've got to get off your bottom and start making some moves, and stop crying in some corner about why you are where you are. Truth be known, no one really wants to carry your burden and they probably don't have the time or resources to carry you through it all; it's your life, so own it and own your purpose. It's your obligation to your family, job, and market to be successful, and create business for whatever cause you represent. Be an ambassador for your company and I encourage you to live and breathe your Value Proposition.

The 3-Tiered framework is exceptionally powerful, and intended for a very specific type of person, business and brand. If you're someone who would love to bring people together and lead them to a prevailing outcome, then you're likely a fit. If your business or brand is one that is genuinely "mission-driven" or you know you can find a way to bring an unpretentious sense of mission into it, then it's likely right for you. If the pain or problem you're looking to solve (or already solve with your business or brand) is shared among many, and not unique to a few, then it's crying out for this strategy.

If you have interest in inspiring large numbers of people to make something big happen, if your business or brand serves a widespread shared pain or problem, then it's likely the type of business or brand that can tap the basis to fuel rapid growth and mass response. Why is this so important? Because there are tons of ways to build an old-school, modest-growth businesses. There's nothing wrong with that. Slow growth, nourishing a basic consumer need and focusing more on selling than inspiring is fine for some.

However, to grow a revolutionary business, to be able to move large numbers of people to briskly help you build your dream, evangelize your brand, buy your solutions and make a difference, there has to be something bigger at play—a bigger mission, shared pain and a willingness to lead. Is that you and your business? You're the one who decides. People who do things that matter don't sit and watch the world pass by. They MAKE the world they envision happen. Let's do this together!

To give clarity to this model, I've personally built my #1 business model around it for the automotive industry. I find a market, choose a Spotlight Dealer of the area, partner them with a local charitable organization, and showcase them both by putting on a first time ever 3-tiered Community Event. It's an event where everyone in the market wins, the dealer, the charity, and the buying public. I get local news media to pick up the story and I do response-marketing approaches to get thousands of people to respond and act on the event. I also provide the dealership with Virtual Training Certification courses, closing workshops, and daily training and motivation so they are in the "Get it Club" before the event even starts. I also educate and motivate the public to take action and get the local charity to advocate the event and do geo-targeted campaigns and marketing to help support the cause. I build a movement with a cause, create a grass-roots approach, and reward the dealer and charity with a presentation at the end of the event. The results produced satisfy the dealer with a month's worth of sales in only 5 days and the charity gets their local message out as they earn thousands for their initiatives. I have been able to create a whole brand around this, called Spotlight Dealers of America, finding dealers who will wear the badge of "For the Community" Spotlight Dealer.

Ok, so let's plunge into this and I want you to understand that this is a very straightforward strategy. One that anyone who is passionate enough and has that "do whatever it takes" attitude, can get this done. If you're in a company that is selling something, anything, and it needs to hit a certain threshold of product or services or budget, then start using this art of revolution to get that proverbial shot in the arm you're needing to be successful.

> I. It starts with Promotion and Pain.
> II. Instruction and Preparation, . . . and finally,
> III. The execution and performance.

Master these three steps and you will build wealth. Here we go, grab your highlighters and notepads, buckle your chin strap, and let's get ready to have untold power with the *3-Tiered Comprehensive Sales Approach*.

1. Creating the buzz and steam in The Marketplace

Let me ask you an important question. Can the core ideals of political revolution be applied in a consumer context to both empower large numbers of people to act AND launch or grow a company, product, or brand? I have proven that it can, and with this first step of finding your message and building your movement you have to be able to announce the pain, leverage the pain, and solve the pain, get mad and get a message for people to get behind and build your rally-cry during your first phase of marketing your event, product, business, or whatever your cause is. You must tell the story and scream it out loud and that you or your company has a problem solving solution. Get the needed buy-in, get them drinking the 'cool aid' because you're marketing to masses of people; people see a moving line and get in it. This is about people-work not paperwork. Have compelling offers and create an event people will get behind and be proud of.

Remember, some people are motivated by seeing the light, but most are motivated by feeling the heat. If you have the resources, try to use mass media, direct media, charity advocating, Social Media, and viral marketing, and build a local, national, or global army working "for the cause." Make a wave and then ride it with a movement or a crusade by building a branded event or promotion around it. Put the Spotlight on the person or company or product doing the 'fixing' and leading the charge and showcase them or it; turn them or it into a star – a new hope for the communities.   This step is all about laying the foundation early and making your promotion or revolution birth it's buzz in the marketplace, and to gain the steam to sustain longevity to reach the required goals. This is a softening of the ground approach, and the initial roll out and full media outlay is ready to be fired with multiple bullets.

2. Educating and training

As the experts say, *the more you sweat in training the less you bleed in battle,* so make sure everyone involved or is instrumental in the success of the campaign is ready. But before training, it takes understanding and a shared sense of ownership in the outcome which fuels bigger action. First, start by empowering your troops with knowledge, support, tools, and access. Provide a powerful, emotional rally point, help harmonize and focus their behaviors, and help them to craft their story and messaging to their clients. Getting them to completely drink the 'cool aid' and buying in is very important to start momentum, and we all know momentum is easier to steer than it is to start.

You have to get everyone to collapse their own comfort zones and challenge the status quo for your agenda to not only stay on course, but to get it kick started with a bang, and of course, to end with a boom. Salespeople or associates will come together around a shared emotion, so tap into those emotions with your rally-cry and problem-solving agenda. Identify your "Toward" vision by creating a clear, specific vision for their NEW REALITY and build your resonant story by naming and defining it. By crafting your manifesto, you bring your tribe together with unifying beliefs.

Who the Dictator or Director will be to lead everyone is crucial in your success. *A fish rots from the head down,* so you have to have a strong leader and person of influence managing everyone's moves, but someone who is one of us—humble, vulnerable, and decisive. Create a timeline, goals, and training curriculum so everyone involved will be singing from the same sheet of music. Before executing your plan, everyone needs to have understanding, buy in, and the ability to do their job, whatever their role is. Communication and role-play is everything during this phase.

The 2nd Tier integrates elements from educating everyone on evangelist growth mechanics, social technology, response-marketing strategies, behavior-change, story-architecture, and social-dynamics. This is normally an engineered plan, not natural, so all involved will have enough time to prepare. Round table meetings, conferencing, training, and goals are a great start. When it comes to setting your goals, use the baseline/brass ring method. A Baseline Goal is good enough, the essential numbers or results that need to be met as an individual or by the whole. The brass ring goal is hitting it out of the park, superseding baseline, or extraordinary results. Have everyone set their baseline and brass ring before execution and make sure everyone knows the core-values of the business model.

For my dealerships, it usually starts with five basic core values:
#1. Market-share
#2. Margin
#3. CSI
#4. Community Embracement
#5. A well-trained staff

My whole vision is based around gaining them more market share, increasing their margins or gross profits, guiding them to do business at the highest level of integrity and satisfaction of their customers. My vision includes getting the local community involved by creating compelling offers, movements, and retention, and finally, always providing the most advanced training skills to catapult them to another level of sales success.

3. Execution

Up to this point, you've built your movement, created the buzz in the market place, rallied your troops, trained everyone, and everyone knows their roles. You, your core leaders, sales reps, evangelists and educators are now ready to execute your event or campaign.

At this point you should have multiple channels running at once, but one main home base. At the home base, you've created mechanisms to track action, results, and milestones. You can't manage what you don't measure, so make sure every important moving part is logged. From intenders, responders, call-ins, electronic registrations, appointments set and showed, foot-traffic, demos, write-ups, and orders, or whatever is specific in your field, make sure it is reported. Your team has to stay in attack mode, casualness leads to casualties! During this final stage, you want to create an environment that compels people to act over and over again.

An environment that supports the cause is of ease, with options and swiftness. Your proposals should be so good, so lopsided in terms of value, so void of any risk, that your customers would think to themselves "Why wouldn't I do this?" Your proposal should focus on five important elements:

a) The features and deliverables
b) The benefits
c) Pricing
d) Terms
e) The risk reversal element

You want to ask them for their business with logic and confidence. Of course, before asking them for their business, you have to remove all the obstacles, or otherwise turn stumbling blocks into stepping stones. If they believe they are getting immense value from you and you understand their problems with pinpoint accuracy, and that your product, company, or movement is a giant breakthrough for them, then your chances of gaining them are greater because of the 3 Tiers and the "Now" environment they are in. In this final stage, let there be a celebration, recognition, rewarding, and one final come together to set in stone and announce the accomplishments of your sales revolution.

To conclude here, people who learn and master the core elements of *The 3-Tiered Comprehensive Sales Approach* serve and impact more people on a deeper level, magnify reach, and better empower individuals to create their own realities with a fraction of the effort and cost. Look, some people dream of success, while others wake up and work hard for it. We have to sow our seeds to reap our harvest and I realize these strategies may be a bare knuckles approach or politically incorrect, but nonetheless, they are easy to understand and are ready for immediate application.

Give the world or your communities something to believe in and something to belong to by building something that matters. People have an overwhelming desire to believe in something. Become the focal point of that desire by offering them a cause, a new path to follow, or rally to get behind. Emphasize enthusiasm and be full of promise and watch your new belief system or movement bring you the untold power you've always been searching for.

About Roe

Roe Hubbard, is a best-selling author, Spike TV and A&E celebrity Automotive Sales host, the Leading Expert Trainer and Promoter for retail car business. He is also the founder of the #1 endorsed sales event company in America – Members Only Automotive – also known as The MOA Group, which is an elite group of Spotlight Dealers showcased in the U.S.

For mass media, he's featured his Spotlight Dealers of America in major publications such as *Forbes, USA Today,* and *The Wall Street Journal,* and has national coverage on Fox, ABC, NBC, and CBS.

Roe Hubbard created and founded the "For the Community" Spotlight Dealer Program, the 1-week Community event, with a Spotlight Dealer Host, partnered with a local Spotlight charity, and features them on over 150,000 *Car & Buyer* magazines, with local news media coverage for direct media and promotion. This program has produced millions in additional profits for his Spotlight Dealers and has raised hundreds of thousands of dollars for Spotlight Charities and local non-profit originations.

Roe is also a Mega-Speaker/Trainer for the automotive industry, and helps thousands of sales departments across the country reach their goals.

Roe lives in Chicago, IL, is married to Brittany Hubbard, and has two sons, Mason and Landon, and two daughters, Julia and Avery.

He dedicates his work to his father who passed away in Oct 2015, Johnny "Hub" Hubbard.

"Hub Up!" ~ Roe Hubbard

CHAPTER 19

A WEALTH OF HEALTH

BY TODD OSOSKI

Things were finally starting to really take off and it all started happening around the time I started working on my body, mind and spirit. I changed my diet, my sleeping habits, I started supplementing with vitamins again, I started working out, meditating, and reading scriptures. I wasn't aware of it until it was already happening and these minor changes were really making all the difference for me again. I say again, because I realized there was a pattern in what was happening when I was applying all these things in my life and when I stopped applying these things. It goes way back to when I was a kid in elementary school and how my mom took care of me. My parents always fed me healthy food, never let me drink soda, made sure I went to bed on time, let me go out and play (get exercise), took me to church, and gave me kids multi-vitamins. Things were really good back then and I was never fatigued and I was getting straight A's.

Fast forward to high school and I was still doing all the same things – like going to school every day, working out five hours a day at least, eating healthy, getting decent sleep, taking tons of vitamins and supplements, and going to church. I was at one of the most productive times in my life, I was in amazing shape, I was happy, and was very successful at everything I did. Things were good and I was never really fatigued.

Fast forward three years, I stopped working out, stopped really eating healthy, wasn't taking any vitamins or supplements, wasn't doing anything spiritual, and wasn't really doing anything with my life. I was just turning 21, but I felt fatigued and tired every day, and all I really wanted to do was go hang out with my friends. I lost sight of my goals and at the time there weren't very many jobs available in Las Vegas – so that required job hunting. I wasn't really thinking about my future or thinking about how productive I was. I was extremely unmotivated and wasn't doing anything similar to what I was doing in high school. I had subconsciously started to realize I had let a lot of things get out of hand and needed to change things back to what worked before.

Fast forward another two years, I got this awesome job working in the oil fields. I was working out every day, eating right, taking vitamins and supplements, sleeping right, and everything was going really well. I even moved to a completely different town and started over from scratch. Then I slowly stopped eating right, stopped sleeping right, stopped working out, wasn't doing anything spiritual. I felt fatigued at work every day and my performance slowly fell off. Then eventually I lost my job once again. I lost everything I had worked so hard for and didn't really realize why it had happened. . . again!

Can you see a pattern here? When I stopped taking care of my mind, body, and spirit, everything else seemed to dwindle and fall apart for me. I would gain everything once I started taking care of my mind, body and spirit, then I would lose it all when I stopped. When I stopped, I lost my motivation and drive, I lost my energy to get things done and felt fatigued every day. I eventually lost everything because I couldn't perform like I did in the beginning of it all. I was clueless as to why this kept happening and then it dawned on me! I realized a pattern in what I was doing during my times of gain and loss and what I could do to become successful again.

I quickly made the changes to my diet, my sleep, my exercise routine, my supplements, my spiritual needs, and my work/life balance, then bam! I really started getting motivated again about everything, not just my diet and sleep routine. The motivation I gained from these changes carried over into every part of my life again. Everything started to get back on track and I was on the road to success in no time. . . and I haven't looked back since! The great thing about this is, anybody can do it with a little effort and consistency. That's why I am here sharing this with you so you can be a Master of Success too! I want you to be the best version of yourself and you can do it if you just follow these simple steps:

FIVE STEPS TO BEATING FATIGUE THROUGHOUT THE WORKDAY

- **Eat healthy:** - Eating healthy is one of the most important things you can ever do in your life. Period. Eating healthy not only increases your life span and quality of life in general, but it can really help you beat fatigue throughout the workday, and here's how. When you are putting nutrient dense, quality food in your body, you're giving your body the fuel it needs to function at maximum capacity. So that means, when you are eating healthy, your body has everything it needs and more to sustain a high energy level to blast through the workday and whatever else you have lined up after work. If you aren't eating anything or you're just eating junk food every day, your body isn't getting the proper nutrients it needs to get through the day. Naturally, if you aren't getting proper nutrition in your body, then your body is going to get fatigued because it doesn't have anything to use for energy. So put away your Bon-Bons, your Twinkies, and those little breakfast muffins and cook up some breakfast burritos, eat some oatmeal (not the sugary kind), or do both! So please, do yourself a favor and make healthy choices when it comes to what you put in your body, so you can give your body the energy it needs to beat fatigue throughout your workday with ease.

- **Sleep:** - Now when it comes to battling fatigue throughout the workday, your sleeping habits can either be helping or hindering you. Every single person on earth needs sleep. Some people need more sleep than the average person and some need less. There have been countless studies on sleep and they have come to the conclusion that the average person needs about 7 to 8 hours of sleep to get the full benefits of sleep including recovery and energy. If you are only sleeping a few hours a night, not only are you cutting your life short (studies show sleep habits are linked to longevity) but fatigue sets in much faster in the workday if you aren't already fatigued before the workday starts because of your lack of sleep. So, moral of the story, get the correct amount of sleep for yourself and you could make fatigue a thing of the past.

- **Exercise:** - If you want to feel like a beast through your workday without feeling fatigued, exercise! I cannot stress enough to you the importance of exercise and how much it has to do with your energy levels. Tons of really successful people exercise and reap the many benefits of it. You hardly ever see people that exercise daily get fatigued easily (unless they just finished working out) and there are a few reasons why. When you exercise, you are forcing your body to burn energy and fatigue itself. Your body will naturally adapt to this and build a larger capacity of energy, and gain efficiency in energy-use to sustain these workouts and keep you going for the rest of the day. Your body naturally gets stronger to adjust to the workload you give it. You also build stamina to workout longer and you will recover faster because your body will adapt quite well. Now think about how much exercising will increase your work capacity! If you can get through an hour of high intensity Zumba, some spiritual yoga, an hour or two of pumping iron or a 5k running session, then work should be a breeze! Once again, exercise will increase your lifespan in the same way proper nutrition and good sleeping habits will, so doing this will not only help you eliminate workday fatigue, but you'll live a long, healthier life as well. So get to it and become that super productive beast you were destined to be and leave that pesky workday fatigue in the dust!

- **Vitamins/Supplements:** - Yes, you are going to get a lot of your nutrients from healthy foods, but not everybody is going to eat everything on the food pyramid and get every nutrient they need daily. That's why they made vitamins and supplements! When fighting the war against fatigue, you stand a much better chance at winning when you have everything the body needs. Vitamins and supplements provide everything you need to supplement your diet and make sure you get all the nutrients your body needs. It is important to have consistency when taking supplements to make sure they remain in your blood at all times to feed your body. The more consistent you are when taking vitamins, the better the results are going to be. Make sure to take a good multivitamin at the very least and pick up any extra vitamins that will help you reach other goals you may have. A B-complex vitamin is great for maintaining energy levels and is a great addition to your arsenal in the battle against workday fatigue.

- **Your work/life balance:** - Last but not least, lead a life of balance. It is absolutely critical to lead a life of balance if you want to beat fatigue throughout your workday, your workweek, and throughout your life. When you get done with your work and it's time to go home, leave your work... at work! It's easy to get burnt out on your work if all you do is work. At this point, fatigue can set in quite easily because you're burnt out on work! How can we avoid this? After work, do some fun things like being with your family, spending some time with your significant other, going out and seeing a movie, going bowling with friends, anything... just do something you enjoy. When work starts to take over your life and it is in your every thought for every hour of the day and you're even dreaming about work, it's time for you to reassess your work/life balance.

What is your work/life balance? It's the balance between your work life and your personal life. You may not even realize how off balance your work/life balance is until you really think about it. How do you tell if your work/life balance is off balance? Let me explain how you can find out if your work/life balance is, well... off balance. How often do you think about work when your home? And vice versa? Are you ever really fully in the moment, or are you ever mentally there per se? Are you a big time boss handling everyone else's problems all the time and receiving work- related phone calls during home hours? Have you ever actually drawn out and illustrated the actual time you spend with family and the time you spend working on, well... work? If you think about it... I mean really think about it, where are your priorities exactly?

These are things you need to ask yourself before you can even decide where you are in the balance between work and life. When you discover exactly where you are hanging in the balance, you can then prioritize accurately and put yourself on the right path to a more balanced life. By doing this you eliminate a lot of unnecessary fatigue due to stress and other side effects that come with an unbalanced life.

- **Get spiritual!** - There's something about getting spiritual that really puts your life in balance. Getting spiritual has many meanings and there are many ways of doing it. You can do yoga, go to church, meditate, read the Bible (I highly recommend it, it has many valuable life lessons and it will humble you), and more. Doing something spiritual and connecting with something greater than yourself is one of the best ways to not only become a more productive, centered, and balanced human being, but you could also stumble upon your life's true purpose through doing these things. When you hear about monks going into the mountains to meditate for years at a time, or when you hear about people finding God, or when you hear about people starting yoga classes or reading scriptures and they suddenly find their life's purpose – there is a lot more to it than you may think, and you should at least give it a try. Billions of people tap into spiritual power and find great satisfaction, power, and meaning in these spiritual undertakings; and you could too. When you are feeling balanced (especially spiritually-balanced), workday fatigue will become much less prominent in your life and you will benefit in many other ways as well.

CONCLUSION:

If you want to be successful, you have to take care of your mind, body, and spirit. Being successful doesn't just come to you; you have to go to it! That means you're going to have to work for it and work takes energy. When we are running low on energy, we feel fatigued. When we feel fatigued, we are not at our most productive state and we don't get near as much done. Too many Americans needlessly fight fatigue throughout the workday and don't have to. If we all just changed these five things, we could eliminate the battle of fatigue altogether and really start being productive. We could run through a workday, run a marathon, and come home to cook dinner for the family without ever feeling fatigued like we do right now. Plus, everything I'm sharing with you right now will help you live a longer, healthier life; and if that's not incentive enough to do these things, then I don't know what is! I wish you all the best and here's to you becoming a *Master of Success!*

About Todd

Todd Ososki is an ambitious young man seeking to accomplish what most would refer to as the American Dream. Todd is an inventor, entrepreneur, and now an author with no plans on stopping here. With this book being his first real introduction into the public eye, it is just the beginning of more creative content to come from this young man.

Todd Ososki plans on releasing several more books within the next couple of years along with more of his invention ideas. Currently a business student, soon to be a proud provisional patent owner as well as aspiring business owner, Todd is well on his way to success. When he isn't traveling the countryside as a professional driver for Knight transportation, he's busy chipping away at his business degree online, writing future books, and putting his future inventions into action with relentless ambition.

Todd is a young man on the rise moving in fast forward to success.

CHAPTER 20

THE ONLY WOMAN IN THE ROOM
– GETTING THE OPPORTUNITY YOU DESERVE

BY ANGELIQUE BOCHNAK, Ph.D.

The reality of gender gap and inequality in our society is just as real today as it was 100 years ago. Granted, 100 years ago, a life for a woman looked very different than it does today, but that doesn't make the issue any less real. Today the issues surrounding gender gap and inequality are focused more on women's roles in the workplace and in executive level positions. Unfortunately, solutions to inequality issues like this are never simple and no matter how far we progress as a society there will always be a few individuals keeping the gender gap alive.

Recently there have been countless articles written and numerous women-movements initiated to try and close the gender gap in the workplace. These articles and initiatives are calling for action from corporations, asking them to open the executive doors to women, demanding that these corporations consider more women for executive level positions. Are these doors really closed to us? In part, yes. But the fault may not entirely be in the lap of corporate America. Before we lay blame entirely on male executive leaders, we need to take a closer look at the decisions women make and why we make those decisions.

First of all, not all women want to be an executive leader. I would argue that a very small percentage of women actually aspire to lead and run major corporations. A large portion of the female population aspire to be stay-at-home moms and we should praise and commend those women for making that decision. Being a full-time mom is a hard job. A lot of women may actually wish they could be stay-at-home moms, but need to work in order contribute financially to the household. Others choose to give up on a career because they can't seem to figure out how to have both. Even fewer woman are determined to have both, to have the successful career and raise a family. These are the women trying to get through the executive level doors of corporate America.

The problem is more often than not we get stuck just outside the doors. We can see the doors and we are trying to get through the doors, but no matter how hard we work, we can't figure out how to break the barrier to jump into executive management. I have always known without a doubt that I wanted to reach the top, to be a leader in my profession. The problem was I had no idea how to get there. There were no practical "how to" guides to show me the way. Even worse, I had no mentor to teach me what I needed to do to reach that level of success.

Through many years of hard work and determination, I eventually managed to reach senior level status. By the time I reached to this level, the gender gap was even worse. More often than not, I was the only woman in the room. With no mentor to learn from and no other women to model myself after, I was left learning how to maneuver through my career by trial and error. Needless to say, I made lots of mistakes, two of which cost me a lot. Once I realized I was making these two critical mistakes and corrected them, I quickly advanced in my career. In a matter of three years, I not only managed to secure a top level position in my consulting firm, I also managed to double my salary simply by correcting these two mistakes.

Mistake # 1: Don't Play the Victim.

My first job in college was working for a major chemical corporation as an engineering intern through my college's cooperative education program. I will never forget how nervous I was preparing for the job interview. I was nineteen years old and barely understood what a chemical engineer did. When I arrived for the interview, my nerves got even worse. I was the only female student there for the interview. In fact, I was the only female in sight. I left the interview feeling discouraged. It didn't go great. I was certain I didn't have a chance at getting this job. Needless to say, I was shocked when they offered me the opportunity. I thought my interview had gone so poorly there was no way I would get an offer.

When I thanked them for the opportunity and stated that I would do my best to not let them down, they responded with this, "While you may not have been the best candidate we interviewed, you did seem like you could adequately do the job and you are a woman, and we need to meet our diversity quota." At the time, I didn't think too much about their response, in fact, I looked at it as an advantage. I was happy I got the job and I intended on working as hard as I possibly could to prove I deserved the job. Little did I know that my reaction to getting this job set the stage for the first half of my career. I viewed myself as a minority in my profession which was not entirely inaccurate. It was at this moment in my life that I came to conclusion that any success or failures in my career was going to be dictated by the fact that I was a woman.

Of course, this mentality was a critical mistake on my part. Instead of giving credit to my hard work and excellent resume, I assumed every job offer I received was driven by the fact that I was a woman. Furthermore, every time I was passed up on an opportunity, I assumed it was because I was a woman. Suddenly I felt like a victim of a horrible wrongdoing. Over and over again, I watched countless opportunities to manage projects or lead teams handed to male counterparts who were less qualified and less talented than I was. And every time I concluded I did not get the opportunity because I was a woman. It was extremely frustrating and I believed that if I was a man, I wouldn't continually be overlooked.

Even after all these years, I still find myself in situations where my colleagues clearly dismiss my contributions because I am a woman. On some level this type of discrimination is always going to happen. Regardless, we have to stop making it about being a woman. As long as we continue to point out the fact that we are women, everybody will continue to notice that we are women. Don't get me wrong. I am not telling you to stop being a woman. You should be proud to be a woman. But under no circumstances should you play the victim. Consider for a moment how hard you worked to complete your education and build your resume. Why would you want to cut yourself short and undermine your experience?

Mistake #2: Tell Them What You Want.

At a recent town hall meeting for my company, a female colleague asked a remarkably brave question. She wanted to know what the company's plan was to address the lack of female vice-presidents and executive leaders within the company. It's was a good question, especially coming from a very intelligent, hard-working, successful female engineer who probably should have already been promoted to vice-president. The answer was vague but did suggest the executive board was discussing the disparity and working on a solution. He also said that they had no intention of promoting a woman to vice-president just because she was a women. She would have to earn the promotion just like a man. Fair enough.

I am not surprised by the lack of female vice-presidents in my current company. I work in a male dominated profession. There are too few women trying to make it to the top in science and engineering. This kind of change takes time. The problem isn't earning the promotion. The problem is being recognized and noticed for the right qualities and traits and vocalizing your goal to reach that level of success in the company.

No one can read your mind. If you do not vocalize your career aspirations to your boss how will he or she know what your goals are? I left a previous place of employment because after five years of hard work I never once was recognized for my contributions. I was working harder than any of my co-workers and on occasion doing my job and theirs. I thought if I worked this hard and did a great job, they would notice and promote me. When that never happened, I began searching for a new job. Looking back on that position I now see where I went wrong. I never once sat down with my boss and told him what career path I wanted for myself. What I did do is tell him how much I loved my job and how much I appreciated having the opportunity to work on such amazing projects. In his mind I was happy and content just where I was, which couldn't have been further from the truth.

Taking Action

The good news is, avoiding both of these mistakes is simple. Start by listing all the benefits you provide to your company. List your strengths, special skills or training, education, project work experience, and client relationships. Why are you a valuable asset to your company? What would they be losing if you no longer worked for them? What makes you unique? What do you offer that no other employee offers the company?

Write down your goals and aspirations for your career. Is it your goal to become a vice-president within your company? Or maybe you aspire for even more and you want to be the president or CEO. Whatever it is, write it down regardless of your current position. Your current position isn't what matters. What matters is where you want to go. The final step, and maybe the scariest step, is to sit down with your boss and develop an action plan. Share your goals and aspirations with your boss, highlight your skills and unique talents and how they will help you achieve your goals with the company. By taking this approach, you put your boss in a position to tell you what steps you will have to take to achieve that level of success. Ask your boss to help you develop an action plan that can be incorporated into your annual review process. By taking these simple steps you can put yourself in a position that makes it difficult, if not impossible, for upper management to overlook you for advancement opportunities. The best part is your gender has been completely removed from the equation.

Finally, and most importantly, be patient. You will undoubtedly at some point in your career be outwardly discriminated against because you are a woman. Don't focus on the discrimination, focus on your actions and your goals. There is still an overwhelming large number of individuals in the workforce that were raised in very different times than us. Generational gaps can be significant and result in very different viewpoints of what our roles are in society. Take notice, most of the women speaking out about equality for women are from Generation X. Unfortunately, those of us from Generation-X need to be patient and continue to hold true to ourselves. You will run into people, both men and women, from older generations that don't think we belong in leadership roles or don't understand why we want leadership roles. Everybody else is trying to catch up with the fast changing times we find ourselves in. From my personal experience, most male professionals have accepted our place and welcome us in corporate America even though they may on occasion make us feel inferior. Try not to blame them, they are trying to overcome years of conditioning. And yes, they are trying. Remember every generation is different and we are evolving at a very fast rate. The faster we change and evolve, the greater the pain.

It's up to us to be patient, hold true to ourselves and pave the way for future generations, men and women alike. Be so good that they don't even think about the fact that you are a woman.

About Angelique

Dr. Angelique Bochnak is a leading senior scientist for Environmental Consulting and Technology, a leading environmental consulting firm in the State of Florida. Angelique is also an accomplished writer, author, and speaker. Angelique has authored or co-authored numerous well-received technical reports, including published peer-reviewed journal articles. She is often invited to speak at national and local conferences on topics related to her research in ecosystem restoration and empowering women in leadership roles in science and technology. She has guest-lectured at local schools and universities, and taught several college courses on wetland biogeochemistry, soil science and environmental and biological sciences.

Much of Angelique's writing is focused on empowering women to embrace leadership and reach their life goals. More often than not, Angelique has found herself to be the only female professional on her team. With no mentor to learn from and no other women to model herself after, she was left learning how to maneuver through her career by trial and error. After a lot of mistakes and a few successes, she was able to achieve the level of success she desired. Her writing not only shares her experiences, but also provides valuable resources to women everywhere who also desire to achieve success in their careers.

Angelique has authored two non-fiction books. She is expected to release two more non-fiction books in 2016. Angelique is also working on her first fiction novel.

Connect with Angelique:
- Website: www.angeliquebochnak.com/
- Blog: www.angeliquebochnak.com/blog/
- Amazon Author Page: www.amazon.com/author/angeliquebochnak
- Facebook: www.facebook.com/angeliquebochnak/
- Instagram: www.instagram.com/angeliquebochnak/
- Twitter: www.twitter.com/AMKBochnak
- Goodreads: www.goodreads.com/angeliquebochnak
- Google+: www.plus.google.com/+AngeliqueMKBochnak

CHAPTER 21

SEVEN IMPORTANT STEPS FOR COACHING SUCCESSFUL PUBLIC SPEAKING

BY KARL H. JONES, SR.

As a young man and even as a child, I loved to talk and express myself. We moved out of the ghetto to a new area outside of the district, and you guessed it. I blabbed it. I nearly failed 5th grade because of my big mouth. My mom worked for the city and had first dibs on the Summer Jobs available. It was the job of me and my big mouth to *Run Tell That* as Martin Lawrence would say. As I grew up and learned things on late night TV or from my own experiences from my dad's summer drives, I felt obligated to tell everything.

When I became engaged to my wife, I felt a call to my purpose as a minister. Still afraid to speak to strangers, I felt a passion to share the truths I had learned with others. I worked as my Pastor's assistant for three years before I was to preach and teach the Bible. I stepped up and did feel ready, but coaches and mentors know when you don't know that you are ready.

One day while working at a storage facility, I had a chance meeting with a woman who saw not just a talker, but a person who could do sales.

As I quickly found out, just because you are a good talker doesn't make you a good salesman, as Tom Hopkins says. Before you know it, I was in a two-week-long training class. They delivered to each of us this large binder, which was our 'Bible' and Guide book. There were dozens of products given to us to match those in the binder. I felt very intimidated by all the things given to me.

We began by learning about the authors and their products and services. The binders had scripts. Each script gave us stories and specific introductions on the clients as well as the products.

We had to come to work in our suits and ties so we could feel professional; it seemed silly, but it did make you feel so. We practiced those scripts in role playing so much, it was almost nerve-racking. But we began to internalize it. I used the products and developed a passion for them even to this day. The binder included stories of how the products helped people. As I used them, I gained a sense of confidence to sell them as I created my own experiences.

I shot out well into sales, but fell on my face. They helped me back up – I'll tell you how later. Not only did I master the selling process, I was promoted to be a trainer. I also worked as a manager and at one time as an admin. assistant. Wearing all these hats gave me an awesome holistic view and perspective of the business of sales and presenting. We were located in the World's Top Self-Development Company Building (Nightingale Conant). Every month I acquired and studied dozens of programs on cassette at that time. . . lol.

The billionaire owner opened the door so we could run infomercials from home. I did and made over $1,000 plus, only working Friday, Saturday and Sunday. My Daddypreneur adventure started. Later, I started selling on eBay and Amazon, earning hundreds of dollars over a weekend.

After working from home and spending time as a stay-at-home Daddypreneur, I jumped back into the work force when my cash flow slowed down. I worked for two cable companies, an energy company and a lawncare service, and knocked on about 17,000 doors over a three year period.

SEVEN STEPS THAT FUELED MY SUCCESS AND THOSE I TRAINED IN PUBLIC SPEAKING

1. Poise

Realize that people will judge you before you open your mouth. The way you dress speaks silent volumes to people.

The way you dress symbolizes authority or lack thereof: Policemen, Firemen, . . . even in commercials when a doctor is a spokesman, when they are interviewed they more often than not wear a white coat.

As a speaker, how you dress should match your audience and be one step above, but not over-dressed. Watch Presidential candidates – they will all roll up their sleeves when they visit power plants or factories. Why? . . . to appear they can relate to the common man. I teach clients to learn how to speak, because no one has ever seen great speakers looking down and reading a whole speech.

For public speaking, ladies should dress conservatively. Men's suits should be conservative as well. Shoes, survey says, make the man. Choose wisely with help. Copy how other speakers look. Make sure it matches your Brand, at least until you find your own.

2. Your Introduction - Best done by someone else

Preferably have the top executive or most respected person present introduce you. Their credibility is loaned to you subconsciously by the listener who respects that person. We've been taught at an early age when you speak about good of yourself, our Bragger Meter goes off and we judge and say in our minds, "yeah right!" As your accomplishments are mentioned, they need to be positioned to mirror the needs of the audience you are to speak to. Speak of the problem! When I sold lawn care, I led potential clients to the problem on the grass as I painted a picture of the perfect lawn, and my company was the answer to this dilemma I just revealed.

3. Telling Your Story

Above I presented my story of how I found a speaking career and how I achieved success, and how anyone who takes these steps will as well. In telling your story, there needs to be researched, tried and tested facts which anyone can relate to. The impact of stories is the bread-and-butter of all successful sales organizations. When I was doing phone sales, I would tell stories about the products and services – what they have done for my family, my friends and me. As children, we got storytime as a part of the American Middle School system – so there should be no mystery there. ONCE UPON A TIME is a TOP-RATED TV SHOW. The fabric of those stories were to shape our society and the character of those who heard them. The Founding Fathers of America painted a picture of a land where they could come and worship freely.

Telling a good story is one of the best ways to connect with people. JFK created the modern day NASA program. He painted a picture of the U.S. going into Space and getting to the moon first. We accomplished that and the rest is history. Then there was the inspiring Martin Luther King *I Had a Dream* speech. Then it was said Einstein could make smart people feel dumb when he spoke. Steve Jobs told stories as to why we would live better if we got his latest Apple device to help us. He never dressed in a suit when giving his presentation. He made sure he was relatable. Telling stories should paint the picture to the point where people will ask you how much or can I start now?

4. Passion and Compassion

Passion is something you have or you don't have. Passion is needed to bring a sense of the authentic to your presentation. Your enthusiasm will be contagious. Find a subject you are passionate about and deliver that subject with passion. What gets you angry, what makes you happy, and what has helped you that you want to see help others? When you see top speakers you get a sense of their desire to present their content in a way that you'll get it, and make a real change in your life.

5. Self Confidence

Your ability to believe in your message and your ability to present it will be one of the greatest factors in your success in giving a successful speech. Tons of books are written on self-esteem.

I call it the false-esteem movement to reward students with participation trophies. One NFL player had his son give one back.

Real self confidence comes from practice, practice, practice. To know what you are passionate about, inside and out, will give you confidence.

All elite speakers seem to speak effortlessly because of years of presenting. Join Toast Masters and join a MeetUps so you can practice and get feed back from non-customers and clients who will help you tweak your speech.

6. The Close
Your close should go with a bang! Your bang should be tied in with what you told them. Your opening and close. Your audience should feel they got something of value they can use instead of feeling they sat through a commercial or sales pitch. We always teach that when you close, you remind them of the great decision they made. Top speakers always remind the audience of the choice they made and congratulate them for stepping up to their new and brighter future.

7. Mentors
One overlooked but very important factor in the success of most great people is that they have mentors. From the ancient Greek philosophers to Oprah. Oprah speaks of her mentors, Barbara Walters, and of course, Maya Angelou, when she was alive. Oprah went on to mentor Dr. Oz, Dr. Phil, . . . and many others. Then, the greatest athlete to breathe modern air, ever born of woman, was Michael Jordan. One commentator said he had a coach who was an inspiration, as he was cut from the basketball team in high school. He worked hard because it was his passion to play the game he loved.

When I first jumped on the phone I did ok, but I got fired. Then they said, "Hey Karl!" as I was digesting my failure, "We've got a Coaching Program to help people who we believe need extra help to achieve." The rest is history. I became a top salesman and was invited to be a trainer, all because I was coached. The concept of 'show me as you tell me' I use with my clients when preparing them for my TV show. I worked in person with people who were getting ready to present, sell or preach. I also mentored one lady totally by phone, helping her to create her first sermon from scratch, as well as how to be ready to speak in front of the whole church.

Use these seven steps and become a successful public speaker!

You can do it!

About Karl

Karl H. Jones, Sr. coaches professional clients, specializing in those transitioning from corporate to entrepreneurial careers. Karl worked his way up the ranks working for renowned billionaire infomercial king, Kevin Trudeau, culminating in his ultimate position as a Corporate Trainer, he left the corporate world to be a stay-at-home dad and entrepreneur. While creating an online presence for his new coaching business, he chose to focus on helping clients create facility in delivering speeches and presentations, and also preparation for stage or television appearances and performances, which at the time seemed to be missing in most speaker training. Karl also co-created a script for a national campaign with a major telemarketing company.

Through his vitality as a Daddypreneur, Karl formed the philosophy that anyone can be successful given the right circumstances and opportunities. He believes that it doesn't matter what walk of life you are from, he believes in your ability to succeed and wants you to believe in yourself. Karl's Mission is to partner with individuals to build their personal mission statement, business strategy, platform, and income, as they start a business, with his primary focus on fathers.

Using his television show, *Wisdom For Life,* as an idea showcase, Karl provides clients with a vehicle to reach and inspire a potential new customer base. Among his successes as a Business Coach are clients who have gone back to school and pursued the career they had always felt called to. His clients range from those in the public sector to veterans, educators, motivational speakers, entertainers, and sales people. One of his greatest joys is seeing individuals use their potential and gifts, in addition to translating "everyday" skills to business abilities.

Karl H. Jones, Sr. is a Media Correspondent, Television Show Host, Speaker, Trainer, Coach and Mentor. He was trained by industry leaders including Infomercial King Kevin Trudeau, Relationship Expert Ellen Kreidman, Memory Expert and Top Salesman Blaine Athorne, and phone sales expert, John Jacobs, to name a few. He pours his heart and energy into Mentoring and Coaching all those who desire to have a profound, positive change in their lives. Those who create the biggest effect in the marketplace are praised as those who can best communicate effectively.

An Instructor at the Joseph Business School in Oak Park, IL, Karl is in the process of creating a series of original courses for the students. Karl's Boot Camps, 8-week Speaker Academy and Tele-Seminars are held across the country. As the host of his own inspirational television show, he is currently creating a Business Talk Show to present to major television networks. In addition, Karl is also creating a 1-year "Get On TV" Mentorship Mastermind Group.

You can contact Karl at:

- https://speaker-success-training-courses.myshopify.com/admin/products
- http://speakermatch.com/profile/karljones/
- https://about.me/karlhjonessr9
- karlhjonessr.com
- www.cashsaverworldwide.com
- Facebook.com/karlhjonessr

CHAPTER 22

THE FOUR CORNERSTONES TO FINANCIAL FREEDOM AND PROSPERITY

BY JOHN HALTERMAN,
CERTIFIED WEALTH STRATEGIST, AIF, CHFEBC, CEP, RFC

*Gain may be temporary and uncertain; but ever while you live,
expense is constant and certain.*
~ Benjamin Franklin

For more than 20 years, I have noticed a significant increase in the amount of income being earned by the upper middle class. Once upon a time, only the rich could obtain millionaire status. However, with higher incomes, the opportunity for the middle class to become a millionaire is obtainable with smart decisions and hard sacrifices. Still, even if you are fortunate enough to achieve this status, it may not make you feel rich. Why is that? It comes down to security—or a lack thereof. People are insecure about if their money will last as long as they will.

THE UPPER MIDDLE CLASS'S STRUGGLE TO FIND FINANCIAL FREEDOM

Most people have very good intentions when it comes to their financial future. Who doesn't want to achieve financial freedom and prosperity that lasts long after you retire? Unfortunately, intentions do not always lead to successful results, despite our best efforts.

For many individuals, they learn far too late in life that they are not on the fast track to financial success, even when they assume they are. Here are four reasons why:

1. **The responsibilities of personal finances have shifted:**
   The days of retirement pensions are mostly gone, and for good reason. Few companies can afford to pay benefits for 20 to 30 years on employees who are no longer productive for them. It's not financially feasible, therefore, it's no longer an option.

2. **We live in an instant gratification society:**
   Instant gratification...we want what we want when we want it. In today's world, most of us see or want something, and we go out and get it without thinking. When you get that sudden boost in income, are you going to save it or buy yourself something shiny and new? Life gets even more complicated when we add in busy schedules—shuffling our families from here to there, having fun, and simply living the American dream. We get caught up in today without thinking about tomorrow.

3. **The media and sales people create confusion:**
   The media and sales people aim to bring out emotions. Their job is to get you to buy in to their product or service, and we, as a society, fall for it day in and day out. We become headline-driven, causing emotions to surface and irrational thinking. We make decisions based on our initial thoughts and perceptions from that quick sound bite because it's highly influential and compelling. To say the least, they're doing their job. Run from anyone that wants to sell you something for their sake. It's your money, your dreams.

4. **No fiscal education:**
   Most of us spend a great deal of time training and educating ourselves toward making more money and/or being a more productive employee. This is great, but how about fiscal education? The majority of the population is not educated on this equally important matter. Think about it, how many classes have you had on what to do with your money? This is a huge deal because it doesn't matter if you make a lot of money if you don't know what to do with it once you get it.

DON'T WING IT, TAKE CONTROL

You can choose a path to reaching your financial dreams that can effectively navigate the detours and potholes that may come along the way.

You may be living great during your working years, but suddenly find that you have nothing later in life. Maybe your money wasn't as secure as you thought, or maybe you ran out of money altogether. This is a scary thought, but it doesn't have to be.

Do you want to feel more confident about your financial situation? This thought alone can be very daunting, but I have one piece of advice: DON'T WING IT. It's your turn to take action and take back control of your money. We can give ourselves the same security that we used to believe our employers would provide us throughout our entire lives.

People work hard for their money and they have every right to expect that their money should work hard for them, as well as those who help guide them on how to properly allocate it. Financial decisions made today will impact what happens to you when you're in your 60s and beyond.

At Beacon Wealth Management, I begin connecting with people, one at a time, and showing them the processes that will inform them, help them make better choices, and give them the confidence to know they've got it covered—to know they will not run out of money years before they run out of time.

UNDERSTAND THE PROCESS BEHIND THE WEALTH STRATEGY

In order to achieve the end dream, you must first know the steps in between. We organize the strategy development process into four steps:

1. **Discover why money is important:**
   Each family is unique and is treated individually—there is no cookie-cutter strategy. We listen and determine why money is important to your family, starting with the end dream in mind. By having a clear understanding of what you believe your future holds, we can better understand where you want to go. Once we understand why money is important to your family, it becomes the center of all of our financial decisions.

2. Perform a deconstruction analysis:

There is no substituting this step or negating it. We have to deconstruct your current situation to identify gaps and issues that are holding you back from reaching your financial dreams.

3. Development of a customized solution:

This action step is designed around the knowledge of why money is important to you and your family and provides you a clear roadmap to your financial future. Because no two situations are alike, our process is geared toward finding the custom step-for-step solution to solving your most pressing problems that keep you up at night, worried about your future and the future of your loved ones.

4. Ongoing monitoring:

Managing your financial affairs is not a one-and-done approach. As life changes, whether it be income or hardships, the way finances are managed must be adjusted to maintain the desired objective.

THE SCENARIO...

You're a fifty-five-year-old couple with three kids and four grandchildren. You have a dream that you'll be able to help fund some of your grandchildren's education and retire at age 65 with 100% of your current annual income. You also want the security of knowing your money will last longer than you.

It's what you've always wanted. However, things don't always go according to plan. Something may happen along the way that challenges your desired objective, whether it's an unexpected death or improper planning. If that happens, don't just put it down to "fate" and give up. You can have a strategy in place to help make your dreams come true, regardless of the unplanned events that life may throw at you.

THE FOUR CORNERSTONES OF FINANCIAL FREEDOM

We divide our wealth strategy into the four cornerstones of financial freedom. Each is an important part of the equation for developing a strong financial future that focuses on why money is important to your family. The only way to achieve your financial dreams is by having a deconstruction analysis completed on all four cornerstones. We analyze the specific details of your finances, relative to your stated objectives. This provides us a baseline of what action steps we need to take. Of course, tax reduction and efficiency is a must and is taken into account for all of the cornerstones.

1. Family Protection

It's all about having adequate protection for when the unexpected happens. We are going to establish provisions in order for your family to maintain its standard of living regardless of what happens in life. These provisions will be established by factors that are relevant to your family and include an analysis of:

- **Monthly cash flow needs:**
  This is where everything starts. It determines the amount of money you need to maintain your standard of living regardless of what happens, whether it's a death, disability, or retirement.

- **Rainy day funds:**
  In the event of a major emergency, we recommend having at least 6 months worth of monthly expenses available in a liquid asset.

- **Health and disability issues:**
  What are your greatest assets? Many people will mention materialistic things, but it's actually your ability to earn an income. If something were to happen, whether permanently or temporarily, provisions must be in place to replace your lost income. No one plans for health issues, but everyone can plan for how to manage them without it being as financially devastating. If you become incapacitated, it is also important to have a Durable and Medical Power of Attorney in place.

- **Death:**
  Again, no one wants this, but despite our best intentions, it is a possibility for anyone who walks amongst the land of the living. If the unexpected were to happen, how does your family maintain its lifestyle? What debt would you want to be paid off? Would you want education for your children to be fully funded? These are all things that must be considered. Once you understand your intentions, it's time to calculate the amount of protection actually needed.

2. Investment Portfolio Management

How you manage your investment portfolio will have a direct correlation to how successful you are in reaching many of your financial goals. One of the biggest mistakes investors make is chasing past performances or hot investments. It takes intense, thorough planning and assessment to make sure you're doing the right thing.

The first key factor in saving money is to determine the purpose of why you want to save. Most people will save money for one of these four reasons:

    i. A child or grandchild's education
    ii. A significant purchase
    iii. An opportunity to start a business in the future
    iv. Retirement

Next, you have to determine how much money it takes to adequately save for your objectives. Then, you'll determine how comfortable you are with investment risk and your timeframe for reaching your objectives. I am amazed how much unnecessary risk people take with investing and they don't even realize it. We recommend stress testing your investment portfolio to determine if it falls in line with your risk tolerance and how it holds up in different economic situations. Taxes and investment losses are some of the greatest enemies of growing money. Determining tax strategy is another important step in successful investing.

Once you have all of these factors organized, it's time to put together an investment allocation strategy. This strategy will be purpose-driven based on known factors that are important and unique to your individual circumstance.

Your life and the markets will change, and so should your allocations over time. With every life-changing event, you should reassess your allocations.

3. Retirement Lifestyle and Income Planning

The journey to retirement and retirement itself is like climbing a mountain—success is not just measured by whether or not you make it to the top of the mountain safely, it's about making it back down safely, as well.

You've spent 30+ years ascending the retirement mountain, sacrificing and saving. You put off things like making substantial purchases and luxurious travel plans just so you could better prepare for retirement and enjoy the benefits of your hard work. Now that you're within 10 years of reaching the retirement summit, you must understand the risks and conditions involved in making your way down the mountain. The physical and cerebral training to get down a mountain is completely different than what it takes to go up. You will now be taking money out vs. making contributions, which could put you in a position to outlive your income. To safely descend on your retirement journey, there are multiple things to consider:

- Establishing an income threshold that you must maintain in order to provide for your desired retirement lifestyle.
- Developing a structured income strategy that assures your money will outlive you. To do this, you must consider the sources that will create your income. Are these guaranteed sources of income? If not, what happens to your lifestyle if you run out of money?
- Rising health care costs.
- Tax laws—they impact roll-overs and income distributions.

By painting a detailed picture of your desired retirement lifestyle and what income sources will provide you a structured income, you gain the ability to put yourself in a position to safely walk down that mountain and maximize enjoyment without worry during your golden years.

4. Family Legacy and Estate Planning

You've worked hard all your life and made the best choices you could to protect and grow your wealth. Now you are getting older and start thinking about the day when it'll be time to transfer your financial legacy to your family. The problem is the government wants to be your main heir instead of your family.

Are you familiar with probate? It's the official proving of your will. It is also the headache that's made worse by the knowledge that anyone can make a claim on an estate. If you set things up correctly, you can have smart asset ownership in place that eliminates probate court and significantly, if not completely, reduces estate taxation.

IN SUMMARY

I believe every day is an opportunity to give a hard-working individual or family the confidence they deserve to make the most of their hard-earned money. I understand that all of this information can be daunting, but through our experience, we've been able to simplify the process to give you that peace of mind you deserve. At the heart of it all, it's about the opportunity to create stability and certainty in a world that isn't always certain.

The four cornerstones of financial freedom are the fundamentals for managing and organizing your financial affairs based on a purpose—your purpose. It's like cleaning out the junk drawer in the kitchen for the first time in 30 years, and finally getting everything in its place. It provides a simple, disciplined process, rather than just an accumulation of stuff in the "junk drawer" with no meaningful analysis of how each affects the other.

A solutions-based strategy and process work because it's just that—solutions-based. If you follow and maintain this process, along with removing emotion and weeding out the media and salesman ploys, you will find yourself making decisions based on your overall objective and motivation for saving money.

Securities offered through Cambridge Investment Research, Broker Dealer, member FINRA/ SIPC. Investment advisory services offered through Cambridge Investment Research Advisors, a Registered Investment Adviser. Beacon Wealth Management operates independent of Cambridge

About John

John T. Halterman is the founder of Beacon Wealth Management as well as a Certified Wealth Strategist, Accredited Investment Fiduciary, Certified Estate Planner, Chartered Federal Employee Benefits Consultants and is a former member of Ed Slott's Master Elite IRA Advisor Study Group. He is also the host of *Solutions 4 Financial Independence*, a weekly segment on WDTV evening news.

As a professional in the field of retirement solutions and holistic wealth management since 1994, John stresses that managing and organizing your financial affairs involves more than just contributing to a retirement account. During the second half of their lives, he understands that his clients are looking at a much more complex set of financial worries. They are now faced with complicated issues such as having a retirement income they cannot outlive, navigating complex tax laws, saving for their grandchildren's education, and leaving a financial legacy behind.

A native of Weston, West Virginia, John has served in the United States Air Force and currently resides with his family in Clarksburg, WV. He and his wife Lisa have been married since 2005 and have three children. John enjoys racquetball and spending quality outdoor time with his family.